# The Good Energy Cookbook

A Complete Collection of Recipes Inspired by Dr. Casey Means' Teachings to Boost Wellness, Maximize Metabolic Health, and Enhance Overall Vitality. | Full Color Edition

### Betty J. Lawson

**Copyright© 2024 By Betty J. Lawson Rights Reserved**

This book is copyright protected. It is only for personal use. You cannot amend, distribute, sell, use, quote or paraphrase any part of the content within this book, without the consent of the author or publisher.

Under no circumstances will any blame or legal responsibility be held against the publisher, or author, for any damages, reparation, or monetary loss due to the information contained within this book, either directly or indirectly.

**Limit of Liability/Disclaimer of Warranty:**

No book, including this one, can ever replace the diagnostic expertise and medical advice of a physician in providing information about your health. The information contained herein is not intended to replace medical advice. You should consult with your doctor before using the information in this or any health-related book.

The Publisher and the author make no representations or warranties with respect to the accuracy or completeness of the contents of this work and specifically disclaim all warranties, including without limitation warranties of fitness for a particular purpose. No warranty may be created or extended by sales or promotional materials. The advice and strategies contained herein may not be suitable for every situation. This work is sold with the understanding that the Publisher is not engaged in rendering medical, legal, or other professional advice or services. If professional assistance is required, the services of a competent professional person should be sought. Neither the Publisher nor the author shall be liable for damages arising herefrom. The fact that an individual, organization, or website is referred to in this work as a citation and/or potential source of further information does not mean that the author or the Publisher endorses the information the individual, organization, or website may provide or recommendations they/it may make. Further, readers should be aware that websites listed in this work may have changed or disappeared between when this work was written and when it is read.

**Manufactured in:** USA
**Cover Art:** DANIELLE REES

**Production Editor:** SIENNA ADAMS
**Production Manager:** SARAH JOHNSON

**Interior Design:** DANIELLE REES
**Art Producer:** BROOKE WHITE

**Editor:** AALIYAH LYONS
**Photography:** MICHAEL SMITH

# Table Of Contents

| | |
|---|---|
| Introduction | 1 |
| **Chapter 1** | |
| **The Power of Good Energy** | 2 |
| The Science Behind Metabolic Health | 3 |
| Dr. Casey Means' Approach to Wellness | 4 |
| Metabolic Health Made Easy | 5 |
| **Chapter 2** | |
| **4-Week Meal Plan** | 7 |
| Week 1 | 8 |
| Week 2 | 8 |
| Week 3 | 9 |
| Week 4 | 10 |
| **Chapter 3** | 12 |
| **Energizing Smoothies** | 12 |
| Berry Almond Smoothie | 13 |
| Delicious Morning Green Cleanser | 13 |
| Basil with Spiced Zing Breakfast | 14 |
| Sunrise Smoothie with Mint | 14 |
| Flaxseed with Strawberry Smoothie | 15 |
| Iced Blackberry with Banana Smoothie | 15 |
| Lime with Grapy Kale Smoothie | 16 |
| Simple Kiwi with Berry Smooth | 16 |
| Super Easy Veggie Smoothie | 17 |
| Classy Spinach with Blueberry Smoothie | 17 |

| | |
|---|---|
| Berry Power Smoothie | 18 |
| Lettuce with Minty Apple Smoothie | 18 |

## Chapter 4
### Nourishing Breakfasts — 19

| | |
|---|---|
| Spinach Egg Scramble On Bread | 20 |
| Peanut Butter Power Oats | 20 |
| Red Pepper and Feta Frittata | 21 |
| Grain-Free Nutty Granola | 22 |
| Pesto Quinoa Breakfast Bowl | 23 |
| Baked Egg Casseroles | 23 |
| Shakshuka Bake | 24 |
| Caprese Breakfast Pizza | 25 |
| Pumpkin Steel-Cut Oats | 25 |
| Sweet Potato and Black Bean Hash | 26 |

## Chapter 5
### Wholesome Lunches — 27

| | |
|---|---|
| One-Pot Pumpkin Pasta | 28 |
| Lemon Herb-Crusted Pork Tenderloin | 29 |
| Mediterranean Beans with Greens | 29 |
| Smoky Herb Lamb Chops | 30 |
| Grilled Veggie and Hummus Wrap | 30 |
| Crispy Zucchini Fritters | 31 |
| Italian Herb Grilled Chicken | 31 |
| Stuffed Turkey Roulade | 32 |
| Greek-Inspired Beef Kebabs | 33 |

## Chapter 6
### Satisfying Dinners — 34

| | |
|---|---|
| Saucy Quinoa with Zucchini, Beans & Olives | 35 |
| Whitefish with Lemon and Capers | 36 |
| Grilled Salmon | 36 |
| Lemon Orzo with Fresh Herbs | 37 |
| Quick Shrimp Fettuccine | 38 |
| Seasoned Tuna Steaks | 39 |
| Chicken Shawarma | 39 |
| Balsamic Black Beans | 40 |
| Cannellini Bean Lettuce Wraps | 40 |
| Crispy Garlic Sliced Eggplant | 41 |
| Lemon-Pepper Chicken Thighs | 41 |
| Lemon and Paprika Herb-Marinated Chicken | 42 |
| Italian Tuna Sandwiches | 42 |

## Chapter 7
### Simple Sides and Salads — 43

| | |
|---|---|
| Chicken, Spinach, and Berry Salad | 44 |
| Creamy Traditional Hummus | 44 |
| Balsamic Mushrooms | 45 |
| Garlic and Herb Zoodles | 45 |
| Roasted Brussels Sprouts with Delicata Squash | 46 |
| Citrus Green Beans with Red Onions | 47 |
| Garlic-Roasted Tomatoes and Olives | 47 |
| Dried Apple Rings | 48 |
| Citrusy Spinach Salad | 48 |

## Chapter 8
### Nutritious Soups and Stews — 49

| | |
|---|---|
| Cauliflower and Broccoli Soup | 50 |
| Butternut Squash Soup | 50 |
| Cauliflower Leek Soup | 51 |
| Tomato Basil Soup | 51 |
| Easy Brown Lentil Soup | 52 |

## Chapter 9
### Refreshing Snacks and Desserts — 53

| | |
|---|---|
| Almond Joys | 54 |
| Twice-Baked Chips | 55 |
| Apple Pockets | 55 |
| Orange Olive Oil Mug Cakes | 56 |
| Stuffed Cucumber Cups | 57 |
| Savory Mediterranean Popcorn | 57 |
| Banana-Nut Bread Bars | 58 |
| Crunchy Flax and Almond Crackers | 58 |
| Herbed Labneh Vegetable Parfaits | 59 |
| Garlic Crispy Smashed Potatoes | 60 |

| | |
|---|---|
| Appendix 1 Measurement Conversion Chart | 61 |
| Appendix 2 The Dirty Dozen and Clean Fifteen | 62 |
| Appendix 3 Index | 63 |

# Introduction

*I've always thought of myself as a pretty healthy person, but a few months back, I noticed something off with my body. I was constantly tired, had these annoying sugar crashes, and was dealing with this weird, almost unexplainable brain fog. It felt like my body was sending me signals, like a car engine light blinking on the dashboard, but I couldn't figure out what was wrong. It made me anxious, really anxious. I'd catch myself spiraling, Googling every symptom, convinced I was headed for some big health crisis.*

*That's when I stumbled upon Dr. Casey Means and her work on metabolic health. I first heard about her from a friend who's a doctor, and then I kept seeing her pop up in articles and podcasts. Her philosophy around blood sugar stability, insulin sensitivity, and how our diets play a huge role in overall vitality really caught my attention. The idea that these everyday symptoms I was experiencing could be connected to how I was eating? It was a total wake-up call.*

*So, I decided to give her approach a try. I started focusing on whole foods, cutting out those sneaky sugars, and paying more attention to how my meals were affecting my energy. It wasn't an overnight miracle, but little by little, things started to shift. The fog cleared, my energy stabilized, and that overwhelming anxiety started to ease.*

*Now, I'm a big believer in this whole "food as medicine" concept. I've been sharing what I've learned with friends, family, and pretty much anyone who will listen. It's empowering to realize that we have more control over our health than we think, and it all starts with what's on our plate. If you're feeling off like I was, maybe it's time to explore this path too. It made all the difference for me.*

### Dedication

*I want to give a huge thank you to my amazing friend and neighbor, Linda. When I was feeling lost and frustrated with my health, Linda stepped in and pointed me in the right direction. She introduced me to the Dr. Casey Means community and the social media outlets where I found exactly what I needed to take control of my health. Linda, your support and thoughtfulness mean the world to me. You've helped me discover a whole new path to wellness, and I'm so grateful to have you in my corner. Thank you for being such a wonderful friend!*

# Chapter 1

## The Power of Good Energy

# The Science Behind Metabolic Health

Metabolic health is like the body's internal engine—it's all about how efficiently we convert food into energy and use that energy to keep everything running smoothly. When our metabolic health is in good shape, we feel energized, focused, and generally well. But when it's off, we might feel sluggish, irritable, or face a whole host of other issues. Two key players in metabolic health are blood sugar balance and insulin sensitivity. Understanding these can be a game-changer for anyone looking to boost their energy levels and overall health.

- Blood Sugar Balance and Energy Levels

Let's talk about blood sugar, or blood glucose, which is essentially the sugar that circulates in your blood and is the main source of energy for your body. When we eat, especially carbs, they get broken down into glucose and enter our bloodstream. Now, this is where things get interesting. If our blood sugar levels spike too high, we get that temporary energy rush—a "sugar high"—but what goes up must come down. That's when we experience the dreaded "crash," leaving us feeling tired, cranky, and hungry all over again.

Think of blood sugar like a rollercoaster: the higher the spikes, the steeper the drops, and the more drained we feel afterward. Keeping blood sugar levels steady helps prevent these highs and lows, giving us sustained energy throughout the day. It's like moving from that rollercoaster to a smooth, flat road—much easier to handle! The trick is to choose foods that don't cause massive spikes. Whole foods like veggies, lean proteins, healthy fats, and fiber-rich options help release glucose more slowly, which means our energy stays consistent.

Also, it's not just about what we eat, but when and how we eat it. Combining carbs with protein or fat, for example, can help slow the absorption of glucose and keep blood sugar levels more stable. And let's not forget about portion control—eating too much of anything can lead to a spike, even if it's "healthy."

- The Role of Insulin Sensitivity

Now, let's dig into insulin sensitivity. Insulin is a hormone produced by the pancreas that helps regulate blood sugar levels. Think of insulin as the key that unlocks our cells so they can take in glucose from the blood to use for energy. When everything is working as it should, insulin does its job efficiently, and our blood sugar stays within a healthy range.

However, if we're constantly bombarding our body with high-sugar foods, our cells can become a bit "numb" to insulin. This is called insulin resistance, where the body needs to produce more and more insulin to get the same job done. Over time, this can lead to higher blood sugar levels, increased fat storage, and even type 2 diabetes. It's like the key (insulin) is still there, but the lock (our cells) has gotten rusty and hard to turn.

Improving insulin sensitivity is about getting those locks working smoothly again. One way to do this is through regular exercise. Physical activity helps cells become more responsive to insulin, allowing them to take in glucose more effectively. Strength training, in particular, can be incredibly beneficial because it increases muscle mass, and muscle tissue is more insulin-sensitive than fat tissue. So, the more muscle you have, the better your body is at managing blood sugar levels.

Eating a balanced diet rich in whole, unprocessed foods also plays a huge role in boosting insulin sensitivity. Foods like leafy greens, nuts, seeds, berries, and fatty fish are all fantastic for supporting metabolic health. And while we're talking about food, keeping an eye on the glycemic index (GI) of foods—essentially a ranking of how quickly they raise blood sugar levels—can help in choosing more insulin-friendly options.

Sleep and stress management are often overlooked but crucial components of improving insulin sensitivity. Poor sleep and chronic stress can throw our hormones out of whack, making our bodies less responsive to insulin. Prioritizing good sleep hygiene and finding ways to manage stress, like meditation, deep breathing, or even a daily walk, can make a huge difference.

## Dr. Casey Means' Approach to Wellness

Dr. Casey Means has been a game-changer in how we think about wellness, especially when it comes to metabolic health. Her approach isn't about quick fixes or extreme diets—it's about understanding how our bodies work and making sustainable changes that boost our energy, improve our mood, and help us thrive.

### KEY PRINCIPLES FOR BOOSTING METABOLIC HEALTH

Dr. Means focuses on the idea that metabolic health is central to overall wellness. Why? Because when our metabolism is functioning well, everything else tends to follow suit—our energy is stable, our mood is balanced, and our risk of chronic diseases decreases. Here are a few key principles she emphasizes:

**Stabilize Blood Sugar Levels**
This is foundational. Blood sugar spikes and crashes can wreak havoc on our energy and mood. Eating a diet rich in whole foods—think lots of veggies, lean proteins, healthy fats, and fiber—helps keep blood sugar levels steady. Avoiding highly processed foods and sugars is key, as these can cause rapid spikes followed by crashes that leave us feeling drained.

**Increase Insulin Sensitivity**
Dr. Means advocates for improving insulin sensitivity, which means your body can effectively use insulin to manage blood sugar. Regular exercise, especially strength training and interval workouts, can help with this, along with a diet low in refined carbs.

**Reduce Inflammation**
Chronic inflammation is a silent troublemaker that contributes to many health issues. Dr. Means promotes anti-inflammatory foods like leafy greens, berries, nuts, seeds, and fatty fish, and advises cutting back on processed foods, alcohol, and anything that could trigger an inflammatory response.

**Prioritize Gut Health**
Our gut is often called our "second brain" for a reason. A healthy gut is essential for nutrient absorption, immune function, and even mood regulation. Including fermented foods like yogurt, sauerkraut, and kimchi, along with plenty of fiber, supports a thriving gut microbiome.

**HARNESSING FOOD AS MEDICINE**

The idea of using "food as medicine" is about more than just filling your plate with random healthy ingredients. It's about making intentional choices that fuel your body, keep your energy steady, and support your overall well-being. When you focus on eating for metabolic health, you'll notice more consistent energy levels, better mood, and improved focus. Here are some go-to ingredients to add to your shopping list:

**Complex Carbs:** Instead of reaching for refined carbs like white bread or sugary cereals, opt for complex carbs like quinoa, sweet potatoes, brown rice, and oats. These take longer to digest, releasing glucose into the bloodstream slowly and keeping your energy steady throughout the day.

**Healthy Fats:** Don't be afraid of fats! Healthy fats from sources like avocados, nuts, seeds, olive oil, and fatty fish (like salmon) provide long-lasting energy and help keep you full. They also help absorb fat-soluble vitamins that are crucial for your overall health.

**Lean Proteins:** Proteins are key to feeling satisfied and energized. Lean options like chicken, turkey, tofu, beans, and lentils help stabilize blood sugar levels and provide essential amino acids that our bodies need for repair and growth.

**Fiber-Rich Foods:** Fiber is your friend when it comes to sustained energy. It slows down digestion, which helps regulate blood sugar levels. Foods like leafy greens, berries, beans, and whole grains are packed with fiber and keep you feeling fuller for longer.

**Hydration Heroes:** Don't forget about hydration! Water-rich foods like cucumbers, watermelon, and oranges, along with plenty of water throughout the day, help maintain energy and keep you feeling refreshed.

# Metabolic Health Made Easy

Navigating metabolic health doesn't have to be complicated. By making smart food choices, avoiding common energy drainers, and planning balanced meals, you can boost your energy and overall well-being effortlessly.

**Avoiding Common Energy Drainers**
Just as there are foods that can help sustain energy, there are also some common culprits that tend to drain it. Here are a few to watch out for:

**Sugary Snacks and Drinks**
Sure, they might give you a quick boost, but the crash that follows isn't worth it. Candy, soda, and even some "healthy" smoothies can be loaded with sugars that spike your blood sugar levels, only to leave you feeling sluggish soon after.

**Refined Carbs**
White bread, pastries, and other refined grains are stripped of their fiber and nutrients, causing rapid spikes and drops in blood sugar. They might fill you up temporarily, but they're not doing any favors for your energy levels.

**Highly Processed Foods**
These often contain unhealthy fats, sugars, and additives that can mess with your metabolism. Think chips, fast food, and pre-packaged meals. They might be convenient, but they can leave you feeling lethargic.

**Caffeine Overload**

While a cup of coffee can provide a nice pick-me-up, too much caffeine can lead to crashes later. It can also interfere with your sleep, which is crucial for energy. Balance your intake and consider other options like herbal teas for a gentler boost.

## MEAL PLANNING FOR METABOLIC BALANCE

Meal planning can feel like a daunting task, but it doesn't have to be complicated. With a little bit of prep, you can set yourself up for success and keep your metabolism humming along nicely. Here are some tips to get started:

- **Balance Your Plate:** Aim for a balanced plate that includes a mix of protein, healthy fats, fiber-rich carbs, and veggies. For example, a grilled chicken breast with quinoa, a side of roasted veggies, and a drizzle of olive oil checks all the boxes. This combination helps prevent blood sugar spikes and crashes.
- **Prep Ahead:** Spend a little time each week prepping ingredients. Chop veggies, cook grains, and portion out proteins. This makes it easy to throw together meals, even on the busiest days.
- **Focus on Portion Control:** Overeating, even healthy foods, can lead to sluggishness. Pay attention to portion sizes and eat until you're satisfied, not stuffed.
- **Include Snacks:** Have healthy snacks like nuts, seeds, hummus with veggies, or an apple with almond butter on hand. These options are great for keeping energy levels stable between meals.
- **Stay Consistent with Meal Timing:** Eating at regular intervals can help keep your energy levels stable throughout the day. Skipping meals or eating erratically can lead to overeating later and disrupt your blood sugar balance.

Understanding Dr. Casey Means' principles of metabolic health can transform the way you approach your well-being. By focusing on choosing the right foods, avoiding energy drainers, and planning balanced meals, you're setting yourself up for sustained vitality and optimal health. With these foundational concepts in mind, we're ready to dive into practical applications. In the upcoming sections, you'll find tailored meal plans designed to keep your energy levels steady and recipes that embody the principles of good energy. Get ready to explore delicious, health-boosting meals that make nurturing your body both easy and enjoyable.

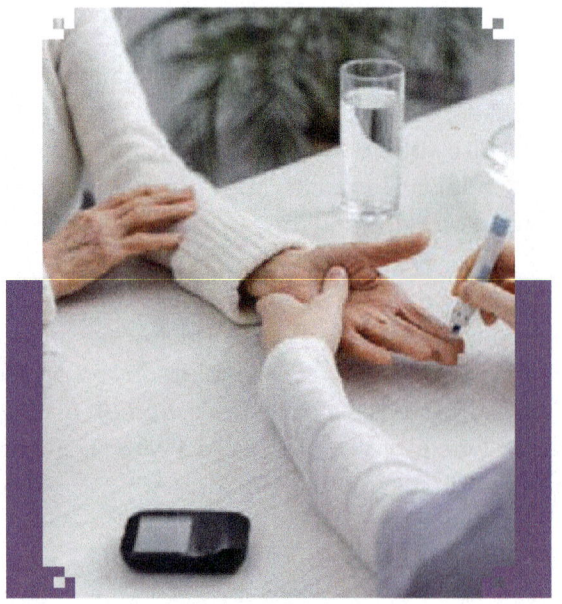

# Chapter 2

## 4-Week Meal Plan

# Week 1

## DAY 1:

- Breakfast: Sweet Potato and Black Bean Hash
- Lunch: Italian Herb Grilled Chicken
- Snack: Apple Pockets (2 Serves)
- Dinner: Seasoned Tuna Steaks

Total for the day:
Calories: 1372; Fat: 77g; Protein: 92g; Carbs: 99g; Fiber: 10g; Sugar: 22g

## DAY 2:

- Breakfast: Peanut Butter Power Oats
- Lunch: Italian Herb Grilled Chicken
- Snack: Apple Pockets
- Dinner: Seasoned Tuna Steaks

Total for the day:
Calories: 1259; Fat: 75g; Protein: 93g; Carbs: 63g; Fiber: 9g; Sugar: 11g

## DAY 3:

- Breakfast: Sweet Potato and Black Bean Hash
- Lunch: Mediterranean Beans with Greens
- Snack: Crunchy Flax and Almond Crackers (4 Serves)
- Dinner: Whitefish with Lemon and Capers

Total for the day:
Calories: 1261; Fat: 65g; Protein: 94g; Carbs: 89g; Fiber: 34.2g; Sugar: 21.8g

## DAY 4:

- Breakfast: Peanut Butter Power Oats
- Lunch: Italian Herb Grilled Chicken
- Snack: Apple Pockets
- Dinner: Whitefish with Lemon and Capers

Total for the day:
Calories: 1245; Fat: 77g; Protein: 86g; Carbs: 63g; Fiber: 9g; Sugar: 11g

## DAY 5:

- Breakfast: Berry Power Smoothie
- Lunch: Mediterranean Beans with Greens
- Snack: Crunchy Flax and Almond Crackers (2 Serves)
- Dinner: Whitefish with Lemon and Capers

Total for the day:
Calories: 1210; Fat: 69g; Protein: 77g; Carbs: 79g; Fiber: 29.6g; Sugar: 23.4g

## DAY 6:

- Breakfast: Sweet Potato and Black Bean Hash
- Lunch: Italian Herb Grilled Chicken
- Snack: Apple Pockets
- Dinner: Seasoned Tuna Steaks

Total for the day:
Calories: 1122; Fat: 62g; Protein: 89g; Carbs: 69g; Fiber: 9g; Sugar: 13g

## DAY 7:

- Breakfast: Spinach Egg Scramble On Bread
- Lunch: Mediterranean Beans with Greens
- Snack: Crunchy Flax and Almond Crackers (2 Serves)
- Dinner: Whitefish with Lemon and Capers

Total for the day:
Calories: 1149; Fat: 57.9g; Protein: 83.9g; Carbs: 80.8g; Fiber: 25.6g; Sugar: 21.4g

# Week 2

## DAY 1:

- Breakfast: Red Pepper and Feta Frittata
- Lunch: One-Pot Pumpkin Pasta
- Snack: Twice-Baked Chips
- Dinner: Italian Tuna Sandwiches

Total for the day:
Calories: 1815; Fat: 42g; Protein: 204g; Carbs: 178g; Fiber: 16g; Sugar: 10g

## DAY 2:

- Breakfast: Shakshuka Bake
- Lunch: One-Pot Pumpkin Pasta
- Snack: Twice-Baked Chips
- Dinner: Italian Tuna Sandwiches

Total for the day:
Calories: 1835; Fat: 40g; Protein: 187g; Carbs: 184g; Fiber: 18g; Sugar: 15g

## DAY 3:

- Breakfast: Red Pepper and Feta Frittata
- Lunch: Greek-Inspired Beef Kebabs
- Snack: Orange Olive Oil Mug Cakes
- Dinner: Italian Tuna Sandwiches

Total for the day:
Calories: 1743; Fat: 66g; Protein: 208g; Carbs: 83g; Fiber: 13g; Sugar: 26g

## DAY 4:

- Breakfast: Shakshuka Bake
- Lunch: Greek-Inspired Beef Kebabs
- Snack: Twice-Baked Chips (2 Serves)
- Dinner: Grilled Salmon

Total for the day:
Calories: 1113; Fat: 49g; Protein: 67g; Carbs: 103g; Fiber: 13g; Sugar: 14g

## DAY 5:

- Breakfast: Red Pepper and Feta Frittata
- Lunch: One-Pot Pumpkin Pasta
- Snack: Orange Olive Oil Mug Cakes
- Dinner: Grilled Salmon

Total for the day:
Calories: 1220; Fat: 52g; Protein: 60g; Carbs: 143g; Fiber: 7g; Sugar: 18g

## DAY 6:

- Breakfast: Red Pepper and Feta Frittata
- Lunch: Lemon Herb-Crusted Pork Tenderloin
- Snack: Twice-Baked Chips
- Dinner: Italian Tuna Sandwiches

Total for the day:
Calories: 1521; Fat: 45g; Protein: 205g; Carbs: 77g; Fiber: 11g; Sugar: 9g

## DAY 7:

- Breakfast: Shakshuka Bake
- Lunch: One-Pot Pumpkin Pasta
- Snack: Twice-Baked Chips (2 Serves)
- Dinner: Grilled Salmon

Total for the day:
Calories: 1304; Fat: 39g; Protein: 55g; Carbs: 186g; Fiber: 14g; Sugar: 11g

# Week 3

## DAY 1:

- Breakfast: Grain-Free Nutty Granola
- Lunch: Grilled Veggie and Hummus Wrap
- Snack: Almond Joys
- Dinner: Lemon Orzo with Fresh Herbs

Total for the day:
Calories: 1356; Fat: 94g; Protein: 32g; Carbs: 110g; Fiber: 21g; Sugar: 17g

## DAY 2:

- Breakfast: Grain-Free Nutty Granola
- Lunch: Grilled Veggie and Hummus Wrap
- Snack: Garlic Crispy Smashed Potatoes
- Dinner: Lemon-Pepper Chicken Thighs

**Total for the day:**
Calories: 1418; Fat: 101g; Protein: 61g; Carbs: 73g; Fiber: 23g; Sugar: 11g

## DAY 3:

- Breakfast: Baked Egg Casseroles
- Lunch: Stuffed Turkey Roulade
- Snack: Garlic Crispy Smashed Potatoes
- Dinner: Lemon Orzo with Fresh Herbs

**Total for the day:**
Calories: 1506; Fat: 71g; Protein: 97g; Carbs: 117g; Fiber: 15g; Sugar: 13g

## DAY 4:

- Breakfast: Grain-Free Nutty Granola
- Lunch: Grilled Veggie and Hummus Wrap
- Snack: Almond Joys
- Dinner: Lemon Orzo with Fresh Herbs

**Total for the day:**
Calories: 1356; Fat: 94g; Protein: 32g; Carbs: 110g; Fiber: 21g; Sugar: 17g

## DAY 5:

- Breakfast: Grain-Free Nutty Granola
- Lunch: Grilled Veggie and Hummus Wrap
- Snack: Garlic Crispy Smashed Potatoes
- Dinner: Lemon Orzo with Fresh Herbs

**Total for the day:**
Calories: 1506; Fat: 92g; Protein: 41g; Carbs: 137g; Fiber: 27g; Sugar: 15g

## DAY 6:

- Breakfast: Baked Egg Casseroles
- Lunch: Stuffed Turkey Roulade
- Snack: Almond Joys
- Dinner: Lemon-Pepper Chicken Thighs

**Total for the day:**
Calories: 1268; Fat: 82g; Protein: 108g; Carbs: 26g; Fiber: 5g; Sugar: 11g

## DAY 7:

- Breakfast: Grain-Free Nutty Granola
- Lunch: Stuffed Turkey Roulade
- Snack: Almond Joys
- Dinner: Lemon-Pepper Chicken Thighs

**Total for the day:**
Calories: 1303; Fat: 95g; Protein: 95g; Carbs: 19g; Fiber: 6g; Sugar: 9g

# Week 4

## DAY 1:

- Breakfast: Berry Almond Smoothie
- Lunch: Smoky Herb Lamb Chops
- Snack: Stuffed Cucumber Cups
- Dinner: Saucy Quinoa with Zucchini, Beans & Olives

**Total for the day:**
Calories: 1298; Fat: 72g; Protein: 60g; Carbs: 100g; Fiber: 26g; Sugar: 28g

## DAY 2:

- Breakfast: Pesto Quinoa Breakfast Bowl
- Lunch: Smoky Herb Lamb Chops
- Snack: Stuffed Cucumber Cups
- Dinner: Quick Shrimp Fettuccine

**Total for the day:**
Calories: 1589; Fat: 88g; Protein: 72g; Carbs: 138g; Fiber: 21g; Sugar: 12g

**DAY 3:**

- Breakfast: Berry Almond Smoothie
- Lunch: Crispy Zucchini Fritters
- Snack: Savory Mediterranean Popcorn
- Dinner: Quick Shrimp Fettuccine

Total for the day:
Calories: 1521; Fat: 85g; Protein: 54g; Carbs: 146g; Fiber: 16g; Sugar: 16g

**DAY 4:**

- Breakfast: Pesto Quinoa Breakfast Bowl
- Lunch: Crispy Zucchini Fritters
- Snack: Savory Mediterranean Popcorn
- Dinner: Saucy Quinoa with Zucchini, Beans & Olives

Total for the day:
Calories: 1338; Fat: 73g; Protein: 37g; Carbs: 133g; Fiber: 32g; Sugar: 22g

**DAY 5:**

- Breakfast: Berry Almond Smoothie
- Lunch: Smoky Herb Lamb Chops
- Snack: Herbed Labneh Vegetable Parfaits
- Dinner: Saucy Quinoa with Zucchini, Beans & Olives

Total for the day:
Calories: 1306; Fat: 73g; Protein: 59g; Carbs: 110g; Fiber: 23g; Sugar: 37g

**DAY 6:**

- Breakfast: Pesto Quinoa Breakfast Bowl
- Lunch: Crispy Zucchini Fritters
- Snack: Savory Mediterranean Popcorn
- Dinner: Quick Shrimp Fettuccine

Total for the day:
Calories: 1818; Fat: 84g; Protein: 64g; Carbs: 206g; Fiber: 31g; Sugar: 21g

**DAY 7:**

- Breakfast: Sunrise Smoothie with Mint
- Lunch: Smoky Herb Lamb Chops
- Snack: Savory Mediterranean Popcorn (2 Serves)
- Dinner: Saucy Quinoa with Zucchini, Beans & Olives

Total for the day:
Calories: 1292; Fat: 72g; Protein: 48.9g; Carbs: 121.9g; Fiber: 26.9g; Sugar: 16.9g

# Chapter 3

## *Energizing Smoothies*

### Berry Almond Smoothie

**Prep time: 5 minutes | Cook time: none | Serves 4**

- 2 cups frozen berries of choice
- 1 cup plain low-fat Greek yogurt
- 1 cup unsweetened vanilla almond milk
- ½ cup natural almond butter

1. Put the berries, yogurt, almond milk, and almond butter into a blender and blend until smooth.
2. If the smoothie is too thick, add more almond milk to thin.

**PER SERVING**

Calories: 277 | Fat: 18g | Protein: 13g | Carbs: 19g | Sugars: 11g | Fiber: 6g

### Delicious Morning Green Cleanser

**Prep time: 10 minutes | Cook time: 0 minutes | Serves 2 cups**

- 1 green bell pepper, de-stemmed
- 1 cup broccoli florets
- 1 cucumber, quartered
- ¼ head cabbage

1. Blend all greens together in the order listed.
2. If you feel it tastes too rich, add a bit more cucumber.
3. All these ingredients work well independently as detoxifiers, but together they create a real powerhouse

**PER SERVING**

Calories: 46.9 | Fat: 0.3g | Protein: 2.9g | Carbs: 9.9g | Fiber: 2.9g | Sugar: 4.9g

## Basil with Spiced Zing Breakfast

**Prep time: 10 minutes | Cook time: 0 minutes | Serves 2 cups**

- 2 green bell peppers, de-stemmed
- 1 tomato
- 4 stalks celery
- 2 basil leaves
- ½ jalapeño pepper, de-stemmed (optional)

1. Blend all ingredients together and enjoy.

**PER SERVING**

Calories: 38.9 | Fat: 0.2g | Protein: 1.9g | Carbs: 8.9g | Fiber: 1.9g | Sugar: 4.9g

## Sunrise Smoothie with Mint

**Prep time: 10 minutes | Cook time: 0 minutes | Serves 1**

- 1 cup chopped romaine lettuce
- 2 medium cucumbers, peeled and quartered
- ¼ cup chopped mint
- 1 cup water, divided

1. Place romaine, cucumbers, mint, and ½ cup water in a blender and combine thoroughly.
2. Add remaining water while blending until desired texture is achieved.

**PER SERVING**

Calories: 39.9| Fat: 0g | Protein: 1.9g | Carbs: 8.9g | Fiber: 3.9g | Sugar: 3.9g

## Flaxseed with Strawberry Smoothie

**Prep time: 10 minutes | Cook time: 0 minutes | Serves 3**

- 1 cup coconut milk
- 1 cup fresh strawberries
- 2 tbsp. flaxseeds
- 1 Greek yogurt vanilla or coconut flavor (5.3 oz.)
- ½ teaspoon stevia (1 packet)
- 1 cup ice cubes

1. Turn on your blender.
2. Blend all ingredients on high for 30 to 45 seconds, or until desired consistency is reached.

**PER SERVING**

Calories: 99 | Fat: 2.9g | Protein: 6.9g | Carbs: 10.9g | Fiber: 1.9g | Sugar: 8.9g

## Iced Blackberry with Banana Smoothie

**Prep time: 10 minutes | Cook time: 0 minutes | Serves 4**

- 1 cup fresh blackberries, or more to taste
- 2 cups crushed ice
- 5 large strawberries, hulled and halved
- 1 teaspoon white sugar, or to taste (optional)
- 1 large banana
- 12 fresh blackberries
- 1/3 cup orange juice

1. Place 1 cup blackberries, strawberries, banana, orange juice, and ice into a blender in that order, and blend on high speed until smooth, 30 seconds to 1 minute.
2. Pour into 4 glasses and top each serving with 3 blackberries for garnish.

**PER SERVING**

Calories: 72.9 | Fat: 0.4g | Protein: 1.3g | Carbs: 17.9g | Fiber: 2.9g | Sugar: 4.9g

*The Good Energy Cookbook*

## Lime with Grapy Kale Smoothie

**Prep time: 10 minutes | Cook time: 5 minutes | Serves 4**

- 4 cups fresh kale, chopped
- 2 cups seedless green grapes
- 3 cups water
- ½ cup ice cubes
- 4 drops stevia
- 2 tablespoons fresh lime juice

1. Add everything in a food processor and pulse until smooth.
2. Pour in serving glasses.
3. Top with crushed ice.
4. Serve with a smile.

**PER SERVING**
Calories: 90.9 | Fat: 0g | Protein: 2.5g | Carbs: 22.6g | Fiber: 1.5g | Sugar: 10.9g

## Simple Kiwi with Berry Smooth

**Prep time: 10 minutes | Cook time: 0 minutes | Serves 4**

- 1 banana, peeled
- 5 strawberries, capped, plus 1 strawberry for garnish
- ¼ cup blueberries
- 4 kiwis, peeled
- 1 small cucumber, quartered
- ¼ cup water

1. Toss all ingredients in your blender and puree until smooth.
2. Pour into glass and garnish with a strawberry.

**PER SERVING**
Calories: 71.9 | Fat: 0.3g | Protein: 1.9g | Carbs: 17.9g | Fiber: 2.3g | Sugar: 10.9g

## Super Easy Veggie Smoothie

**Prep time:** 10 minutes | **Cook time:** 0 minutes | Serves 3

- 1 clove garlic
- ¼ head cabbage
- 1 kale leaf
- 1 beet
- 1 carrot
- 1 stalk celery
- 1 cup water

1. Add all ingredients and blend.
2. If you'd like, add a pinch or two of sea salt for flavor and a mineral boost, or perhaps cayenne for the extra antioxidant pop from the capsaicin.

**PER SERVING**

Calories: 41.9 | Fat: 0.2g | Protein: 1.9g | Carbs: 8.9g | Fiber: 2.9g | Sugar: 4.9g

## Classy Spinach with Blueberry Smoothie

**Prep time:** 10 minutes | **Cook time:** 0 minutes | Serves 2

- 1 cup strawberries
- 2 cups spinach, raw
- ½ cup blueberries
- ½ cup Greek yogurt
- 2 cups of water

1. Add listed ingredients to a blender
2. Blend until you have a smooth and creamy texture
3. Serve chilled and enjoy!

**PER SERVING**

Calories: 87.9 | Fat: 1.4g | Protein: 6.9g | Carbs: 13.9g | Fiber: 2.9g | Sugar: 6.9g

## Berry Power Smoothie

**Prep time: 5 minutes | Cook time: 5 minutes | Serves 1**

- ¼ cup frozen blueberries
- ¼ cup frozen strawberries
- ½ cup baby spinach
- 2 tablespoons unsalted almond butter
- 1½ cups coconut milk or unsweetened nut milk
- 1/8 teaspoon ground cinnamon (optional)

1. Place all of the ingredients into a blender and pulse until well combined, about 1 minute.
2. Pour into a glass and enjoy immediately.

**PER SERVING**

Calories: 359 | Fat: 27g | Carbs: 19g | Fiber: 7g | Sugar: 8g | Protein: 11g

## Lettuce with Minty Apple Smoothie

**Prep time: 5 minutes | Cook time: 0 minutes | Serves 2**

- ½ cup mixed berries (frozen or fresh)
- 10 leaves of mint
- 1 apple (peeled, sliced and seeds removed)
- 5 romaine lettuce leaves
- 20 ounces purified water (use juice if desired)

1. Turn on your blender.
2. Blend this delicious smoothie on high for 45 seconds, or until desired consistency is reached.

**PER SERVING**

Calories: 92.9 | Fat: 0.9g | Protein: 1.9g | Carbs: 21.9g | Fiber: 6.9g | Sugar: 8.9g

# Chapter 4

## Nourishing Breakfasts

## Spinach Egg Scramble On Bread

**Prep time: 10 minutes | Cook time: 5 minutes | Serves 1**

- 1 teaspoon olive oil
- 1½ cups baby spinach
- 2 eggs, lightly beaten
- 1 pinch kosher salt
- 1 pinch black pepper
- 1 slice whole-grain bread
- ½ cup raspberries

1. Inside the small nonstick skillet, add the oil over moderate-high heat. minutes Place the spinach on a serving platter.
2. Clean your pan, set over moderate heat, and crack the eggs into it. Cook, stirring once or twice to ensure equal cooking, for 1-2 minutes, or till just set.
3. Add spinach, salt, and Black pepper, to taste. with toast and strawberries, serve your scramble.

**PER SERVING**

Calories: 298 | Carbs: 20.8 | Protein: 17.9g | Fat: 15.9g | Fiber: 3g | Sugars: 6g

## Peanut Butter Power Oats

**Prep time: 5 minutes | Cook time: 5 minutes | Serves 2**

- 1½ cups unsweetened vanilla almond milk
- ¾ cup rolled oats
- 1 tablespoon chia seeds
- 2 tablespoons natural peanut butter
- 2 tablespoons walnut pieces, divided (optional)
- ¼ cup fresh berries, divided (optional)

1. In a small saucepan, bring the almond milk, oats, and chia seeds to a simmer.
2. Cover and cook, stirring frequently, until all of the milk is absorbed, and the chia seeds have gelled.
3. Add the peanut butter and stir until creamy.
4. Divide the oatmeal between two bowls. Top each serving with half of the walnuts and/or berries (if using).

**PER SERVING**

Calories: 261 | Fat: 14g | Protein: 10g | Carbs: 27g | Sugars: 1g | Fiber: 7g

## Red Pepper and Feta Frittata

**Prep time: 10 minutes | Cook time: 20 minutes | Serves 4**

- Olive oil cooking spray
- 8 large eggs
- 1 medium red bell pepper, diced
- ½ teaspoon salt
- ½ teaspoon black pepper
- 1 garlic clove, minced
- ½ cup feta, divided

1. Preheat the air fryer to 360°F. Lightly coat the inside of a 6-inch round cake pan with olive oil cooking spray.
2. In a large bowl, beat the eggs for 1 to 2 minutes, or until well combined.
3. Add the bell pepper, salt, black pepper, and garlic to the eggs, and mix together until the bell pepper is distributed throughout.
4. Fold in ¼ cup of the feta cheese.
5. Pour the egg mixture into the prepared cake pan, and sprinkle the remaining ¼ cup of feta over the top.
6. Place into the air fryer and bake for 18 to 20 minutes, or until the eggs are set in the center.
7. Remove from the air fryer and allow to cool for 5 minutes before serving.

**PER SERVING**
Calories: 204 | Fat: 14g | Protein: 16g | Carbs: 4g | Fiber: 1g | Sugar: 2g

## Grain-Free Nutty Granola

**Prep time: 7 minutes | Cook time: 25 minutes | Serves 6**

- 1 1/2 cups chopped raw walnuts or pecans
- 1 cup raw almonds, sliced
- 1/2 cup seeds, toasted or roasted unsalted sunflower, sesame, or shelled pumpkin
- 1/4 cup unsweetened coconut flakes
- 1/2 cup coconut oil or unsalted grass-fed butter, melted
- 1 tablespoon maple syrup
- 1 teaspoon alcohol-free vanilla extract
- 1 teaspoon ground cinnamon, or to taste
- 1/4 teaspoon sea salt or Himalayan salt

1. Preheat oven to 300°F.
2. Set a rimmed baking sheet with parchment paper or foil.
3. Add the walnuts, almonds, seeds, and coconut flakes to a large bowl. In a separate bowl, mix the oil with the maple syrup, vanilla, cinnamon, and salt. Pour over the nut mixture, tossing to coat.
4. Scatter the mixture evenly on the prepared baking sheet and bake until golden brown, about 25 minutes, stirring once halfway through. Cool completely.

**PER SERVING**

Calories: 248 | Fat: 25g | Carbs: 6g | Fiber: 3g | Sugar: 2g | Protein: 4g

### Pesto Quinoa Breakfast Bowl

**Prep time:** 20 minutes | **Cook time:** 20 minutes | Serves 4

- 1 cup uncooked quinoa
- 2 cups water
- 1 batch raw healing pesto
- 4 cups leafy greens (arugula, kale, or spinach)
- 2 avocados, to serve

1. In a large pot, combine quinoa and water. Cover with a lid and bring to a boil over high heat. Once boiling, reduce heat to low and crack the lid. Cook for 15–20 minutes until all the water is absorbed. Let the quinoa cool completely before assembling the breakfast bowls.
2. Spread 1 cup leafy greens in the bottom of each meal prep container. Add an equal portion of quinoa to each container followed by an equal portion of pesto. Put on lids and refrigerate. Before serving, add 1/2 avocado, sliced.

**PER SERVING**

Calories: 355 | Protein: 9g | Carbs: 28g | Fiber: 11g | Sugars: 4g | Fat: 23g

### Baked Egg Casseroles

**Prep time:** 10 minutes | **Cook time:** 40 minutes | Serves 2

- 1 slice whole-grain bread
- 4 large eggs, beaten
- 3 tablespoons milk
- ¼ teaspoon salt
- ½ teaspoon onion powder
- ¼ teaspoon garlic powder
- Pinch freshly ground black pepper
- ¾ cup chopped vegetables (any kind you like—e.g., cherry tomatoes, mushrooms, scallions, spinach, broccoli, etc.)

1. Heat the oven to 375°F and set the rack to the middle position. Oil two 8-ounce ramekins and place them on a baking sheet.
2. Tear the bread into pieces and line each ramekin with ½ of a slice.
3. Mix the eggs, milk, salt, onion powder, garlic powder, pepper, and vegetables in a medium bowl.
4. Pour half of the egg mixture into each ramekin.
5. Bake for 30–35 minutes, or until the casserole is set.
6. Let cool slightly before serving.

**PER SERVING**

Calories: 213 | Fat: 12g | Carbs: 13g | Fiber: 2g | Sugar: 4g | Protein: 17g

## Shakshuka Bake

**Prep time: 5 minutes | Cook time: 20 minutes | Serves 4**

- 2 tablespoons extra-virgin olive oil
- 1 cup chopped shallots
- 1 cup chopped red bell peppers
- 1 cup finely diced potato
- 1 teaspoon garlic powder
- 1 (14.5-ounce) can diced tomatoes, drained
- ¼ teaspoon turmeric
- ¼ teaspoon paprika
- ¼ teaspoon ground cardamom
- 4 large eggs
- ¼ cup chopped fresh cilantro

1. Preheat the oven to 350°F.
2. In an oven-safe sauté pan or skillet, heat the olive oil over medium-high heat and sauté the shallots, stirring occasionally, for about 3 minutes, until fragrant. Add the bell peppers, potato, and garlic powder. Cook, uncovered, for 10 minutes, stirring every 2 minutes.
3. Add the tomatoes, turmeric, paprika, and cardamom to the skillet and mix well. Once bubbly, remove from heat and crack the eggs into the skillet so the yolks are facing up.
4. Put the skillet in the oven and cook for an additional 5 to 10 minutes, until eggs are cooked to your preference. Garnish with the cilantro and serve.

**PER SERVING**

Calories: 224 | Protein: 9g | Carbs: 20g | Sugars: 7g | Fiber: 3g | Fat: 12g

## Caprese Breakfast Pizza

**Prep time: 5 minutes | Cook time: 6 minutes | Serves 2**

- 1 whole wheat pita
- 2 teaspoons olive oil
- ¼ garlic clove, minced
- 1 large egg
- ⅛ teaspoon salt
- ¼ cup diced tomato
- ¼ cup mozzarella pearls
- 6 fresh basil leaves
- ½ teaspoon balsamic vinegar

1. Preheat the air fryer to 380°F.
2. Brush the top of the pita with olive oil, then spread the minced garlic over the pita.
3. Crack the egg into a small bowl or ramekin and season it with salt.
4. Place the pita into the air fryer basket, and gently pour the egg onto the top of the pita. Top with the tomato, mozzarella pearls, and basil.
5. Bake for 6 minutes.
6. Remove the pita pizza from the air fryer and drizzle balsamic vinegar over the top.
7. Allow to cool for 5 minutes before cutting into pieces for serving.

**PER SERVING**

Calories: 209 | Fat: 11g | Protein: 10g | Carbs: 19g | Fiber: 3g | Sugar: 1g

## Pumpkin Steel-Cut Oats

**Prep time: 2 minutes | Cook time: 35 minutes | Serves 4**

- 3 cups water
- 1 cup steel-cut oats
- ½ cup canned pumpkin purée
- ¼ cup pumpkin seeds (pepitas)
- 2 tablespoons maple syrup
- Pinch salt

1. In a large saucepan, bring the water to a boil.
2. Add the oats, stir, and reduce the heat to low. Simmer until the oats are soft, 20 to 30 minutes, continuing to stir occasionally.
3. Stir in the pumpkin purée and continue cooking on low for 3 to 5 minutes longer. Stir in the pumpkin seeds and maple syrup, and season with the salt.
4. Divide the oatmeal into 4 single-serving containers. Let cool before sealing the lids.

**PER SERVING**

Calories: 121 | Fat: 5g | Protein: 4g | Carbs: 17g | Fiber: 2g | Sugar: 7g

## Sweet Potato and Black Bean Hash

**Prep time:** 10 minutes | **Cook time:** 25 minutes | **Serves 6**

- 1 teaspoon extra-virgin olive oil or 3 teaspoons vegetable broth
- 1 large sweet yellow onion, diced
- 2 teaspoons minced garlic (about 2 cloves)
- 1 large sweet potato, unpeeled, diced into ¾-inch pieces
- 2 teaspoons ground cumin
- 1 teaspoon dried oregano
- 1 (14.5-ounce) can black beans, rinsed and drained
- ¼ to ½ teaspoon salt (optional)
- ¼ teaspoon freshly ground black pepper

1. In large skillet over medium-high heat, heat the olive oil. Add the onion and garlic and cook for 5 minutes, stirring frequently.
2. Add the sweet potatoes, cumin, and oregano. Stir and cook for another 5 minutes. Cover the skillet, reduce the heat to low, and cook for 15 minutes.
3. After 15 minutes, increase the heat to medium-high and stir in the black beans, salt (if using), and pepper. Cook for another 5 minutes.
4. Divide evenly among 6 single-serving containers. Let cool before sealing the lids.

**PER SERVING**

Calories: 124 | Fat: 1g | Protein: 6g | Carbs: 23g | Fiber: 7g | Sugar: 3g

# Chapter 5

## Wholesome Lunches

## One-Pot Pumpkin Pasta

**Prep time: 0 minutes | Cook time: 25 minutes | Serves 4**

- 1 tbsp olive oil
- 2 sprigs rosemary or a few sage leaves, roughly chopped
- 16oz brown rice pasta, such as penne
- 4 cups water
- 1 tsp salt
- 1 tsp ground nutmeg
- 1¼ cups pumpkin purée
- Cashew parmesan cheese (optional), to serve

1. In a large pot or Dutch oven, heat the olive oil over medium-high heat. Add the rosemary or sage and cook for 1 minute until fragrant. Add the pasta, water, salt, nutmeg, and pumpkin purée.
2. Stir until the pumpkin has dissolved into the water. Cover with a lid and bring to a boil. Once boiling, stir and reduce heat to medium.
3. Replace the lid and cook for 20–25 minutes, stirring every few minutes to prevent the pasta from sticking to the bottom of the pan. When the liquid is absorbed and you can push the pasta from the sides of the pan without seeing liquid on the bottom of the pan, the pasta should be cooked.
4. Divide evenly among 4 meal prep containers and let cool fully before putting on the lids and refrigerating. Serve topped with Cashew Parmesan Cheese, if desired.

**PER SERVING**

Calories: 476|Protein: 9g | Carbs: 92g | Fiber: 5g | Sugars: 1g | Fat: 8g

## Lemon Herb-Crusted Pork Tenderloin

**Prep time: 10 minutes | Cook time: 20 minutes | Serves 2**

- 1 (8-ounce) pork tenderloin
- Zest of 1 lemon
- ½ teaspoon dried thyme
- ¼ teaspoon garlic powder
- ¼ teaspoon za'atar seasoning
- ¼ teaspoon salt
- 1 tablespoon olive oil

1. Preheat the oven to 425°F and set the rack to the middle position.
2. Trim away any of the silver skin from the pork tenderloin, to prevent it from curling while it cooks.
3. Combine the lemon zest, thyme, garlic powder, za'atar, and salt in a small bowl. Rub it evenly over the pork tenderloin.
4. Heat the olive oil in a sauté pan over medium-high heat. Add the pork and sauté for 3 minutes, turning often, until it's golden on all sides.
5. Place the tenderloin in an oven-safe baking dish and roast for 15 minutes, or until the internal temperature registers 145°F. Remove it from the oven and let it rest for 3 minutes before serving.

**PER SERVING**

Calories: 182 | Fat: 11g | Carbs: 1g | Fiber: 0g | Sugar: 0g | Protein: 20g

## Mediterranean Beans with Greens

**Prep time: 5 minutes | Cook time: 10 minutes | Serves 4**

- 1 (28-ounce) can diced tomatoes with basil, garlic, and oregano
- 2 (15-ounce) cans cannellini beans, drained and rinsed
- ¼ cup diced green olives
- ½ cup vegetable broth
- 1 teaspoon extra-virgin olive oil or 1 tablespoon vegetable broth or water
- 4 teaspoons minced garlic (about 4 cloves)
- 10 ounces arugula
- ½ cup lemon juice (about 4 small lemons)

1. In a large saucepan or soup pot, bring the tomatoes with their juices, beans, olives, and broth to a boil. Reduce the heat and simmer for about 10 minutes.
2. Meanwhile, in a large skillet over medium-high heat, heat the olive oil. Add the garlic and sauté until it begins to brown, about 5 minutes. Add the arugula and lemon juice. Stir, cover, and reduce the heat to low. Steam for 3 minutes.
3. Divide the arugula evenly among 4 single-serving containers, then spoon the beans over the arugula. Let cool before sealing the lids.

**PER SERVING**

Calories: 310 | Fat: 4g | Protein: 18g | Carbs: 53g | Fiber: 18g | Sugar: 12g

## Smoky Herb Lamb Chops

**Prep time: 1 hour 35 minutes | Cook time: 10 minutes | Serves 6**

- 4 large cloves garlic
- 1 cup lemon juice
- ⅓ cup fresh rosemary
- 1 cup extra-virgin olive oil
- 1½ teaspoons salt
- 1 teaspoon freshly ground black pepper
- 6 1-inch-thick lamb chops

1. In a food processor or blender, blend the garlic, lemon juice, rosemary, olive oil, salt, and black pepper for 15 seconds. Set aside.
2. Put the lamb chops in a large plastic zip-top bag or container. Cover the lamb with two-thirds of the rosemary dressing, making sure that all of the lamb chops are coated with the dressing. Let the lamb marinate in the fridge for 1 hour.
3. When you are almost ready to eat, take the lamb chops out of the fridge and let them sit on the counter-top for 20 minutes. Preheat a grill, grill pan, or lightly oiled skillet to high heat.
4. Cook the lamb chops for 3 minutes on each side. To serve, drizzle the lamb with the remaining dressing.

**PER SERVING**

Calories: 484 | Protein: 24g | Carbs: 5g | Sugars: 1g | Fiber: 1g | Fat: 42g

## Grilled Veggie and Hummus Wrap

**Prep time: 15 minutes | Cook time: 10 minutes | Serves 6**

- 1 large eggplant
- 1 large onion
- ½ cup extra-virgin olive oil
- 1 teaspoon salt
- 6 lavash wraps or large pita bread
- 1 cup Creamy Traditional Hummus

1. Preheat a grill, large grill pan, or lightly oiled large skillet on medium heat.
2. Slice the eggplant and onion into circles. Brush the vegetables with olive oil and sprinkle with salt.
3. Cook the vegetables on both sides, about 3 to 4 minutes each side.
4. To make the wrap, lay the lavash or pita flat. Spread about 2 tablespoons of hummus on the wrap.
5. Evenly divide the vegetables among the wraps, layering them along one side of the wrap. Gently fold over the side of the wrap with the vegetables, tucking them in and making a tight wrap.
6. Lay the wrap seam side-down and cut in half or thirds.
7. You can also wrap each sandwich with plastic wrap to help it hold its shape and eat it later.

**PER SERVING**

Calories: 362 | Protein: 15g | Carbs: 28g | Sugars: 4g | Fiber: 11g | Fat: 26g

### Crispy Zucchini Fritters

**Prep time: 15 minutes | Cook time: 20 minutes | Serves 6**

- 2 large green zucchinis
- 2 tablespoons Italian parsley, finely chopped
- 3 cloves garlic, minced
- 1 teaspoon salt
- 1 cup flour
- 1 large egg, beaten
- ½ cup water
- 1 teaspoon baking powder
- 3 cups vegetable or avocado oil

1. Grate the zucchini into a large bowl.
2. Add the parsley, garlic, salt, flour, egg, water, and baking powder to the bowl and stir to combine.
3. In a large pot or fryer over medium heat, heat oil to 365°F.
4. Drop the fritter batter into the hot oil by spoonfuls. Turn the fritters over using a slotted spoon and fry until they are golden brown, about 2 to 3 minutes.
5. Remove the fritters from the oil and drain on a plate lined with paper towels.
6. Serve warm with Creamy Tzatziki or Creamy Traditional Hummus as a dip.

**PER SERVING**

Calories: 446 | Protein: 5g | Carbs: 19g | Sugars: 2g | Fiber: 2g | Fat: 38g

### Italian Herb Grilled Chicken

**Prep time: 20 minutes | Cook time: 10 minutes | Serves 4**

- ½ cup lemon juice
- ½ cup extra-virgin olive oil
- 3 tablespoons garlic, minced
- 2 teaspoons dried oregano
- 1 teaspoon red pepper flakes
- 1 teaspoon salt
- 2 pounds boneless and skinless chicken breasts

1. In a large bowl, mix together the lemon juice, olive oil, garlic, oregano, red pepper flakes, and salt.
2. Fillet the chicken breast in half horizontally to get 2 thin pieces, repeating with all of the breasts.
3. Put the chicken in the bowl with the marinade and let sit for at least 10 minutes before cooking.
4. Preheat a grill, grill pan, or lightly oiled skillet to high heat. Once hot, cook the chicken for 4 minutes on each side. Serve warm.

**PER SERVING**

Calories: 479 | Protein: 47g | Carbs: 5g | Sugars: 1g | Fiber: 1g | Fat: 32g

## Stuffed Turkey Roulade

**Prep time: 10 minutes | Cook time: 45 minutes | Serves 4**

- 1 (2-pound) boneless turkey breast, skin removed
- 1 teaspoon salt
- ½ teaspoon black pepper
- 4 ounces goat cheese
- 1 tablespoon fresh thyme
- 1 tablespoon fresh sage
- 2 garlic cloves, minced
- 2 tablespoons olive oil
- Fresh chopped parsley, for garnish

1. Preheat the air fryer to 380°F.
2. Using a sharp knife, butterfly the turkey breast, and season both sides with salt and pepper and set aside.
3. In a small bowl, mix together the goat cheese, thyme, sage, and garlic.
4. Spread the cheese mixture over the turkey breast, then roll it up tightly, tucking the ends underneath.
5. Place the turkey breast roulade onto a piece of aluminum foil, wrap it up, and place it into the air fryer.
6. Bake for 30 minutes. Remove the foil from the turkey breast and brush the top with oil, then continue cooking for another 10 to 15 minutes, or until the outside has browned and the internal temperature reaches 165°F.
7. Remove and cut into 1-inch-wide slices and serve with a sprinkle of parsley on top.

**PER SERVING**

Calories: 397 | Fat: 18g | Protein: 58g | Carbs: 1g | Fiber: 0g | Sugar: 0g

## Greek-Inspired Beef Kebabs

**Prep time: 15 minutes, plus 4 hours to marinate | Cook time: 15 minutes | Serves 2**

- 6 ounces beef sirloin tip, trimmed of fat and cut into 2-inch pieces
- 3 cups of any mixture of vegetables: mushrooms, zucchini, summer squash, onions, cherry tomatoes, red peppers
- ½ cup olive oil
- ¼ cup freshly squeezed lemon juice
- 2 tablespoons balsamic vinegar
- 2 teaspoons dried oregano
- 1 teaspoon garlic powder
- 1 teaspoon minced fresh rosemary
- 1 teaspoon salt

1. Place the meat in a large shallow container or in a plastic freezer bag.
2. Cut the vegetables into similar-size pieces and place them in a second shallow container or freezer bag.
3. For the marinade, combine the olive oil, lemon juice, balsamic vinegar, oregano, garlic powder, rosemary, and salt in a measuring cup. Whisk well to combine. Pour half of the marinade over the meat, and the other half over the vegetables.
4. Place the meat and vegetables in the refrigerator to marinate for 4 hours.
5. When you are ready to cook, preheat the grill to medium-high (350–400°F) and grease the grill grate.
6. Thread the meat onto skewers and the vegetables onto separate skewers.
7. Grill the meat for 3 minutes on each side. They should only take 10 to 12 minutes to cook, but it will depend on how thick the meat is.
8. Grill the vegetables for about 3 minutes on each side or until they have grill marks and are softened.

**PER SERVING**

Calories: 285 | Fat: 18g | Carbs: 9g | Fiber: 4g | Sugar: 4g | Protein: 21g

# Chapter 6

## Satisfying Dinners

## Saucy Quinoa with Zucchini, Beans & Olives
**Prep time: 5 minutes | Cook time: 20 minutes | Serves 4**

- 1 cup uncooked quinoa
- 2 cups water
- 2–3 carrots, about 9oz total
- 2–3 medium zucchinis, about 14oz total
- 1 can black beans
- 16–20 pitted kalamata olives, about 2oz total
- 1 tsp salt
- 1/2 tsp freshly ground black pepper
- 2 cups marinara sauce

1. Rinse the quinoa, and then add to a pot with the water. Bring to a boil over high heat, cover with a lid, and then reduce the heat to low. Simmer for 10 minutes.
2. While the quinoa cooks, prepare the vegetables. Dice the carrots and immediately add them to the pot with the cooking quinoa. Stir and replace the lid. Slice the zucchini into thin half-moons and add to the pot. Stir and replace the lid. Let the veggies and quinoa cook for 10 minutes. While the veggies cook, drain and rinse the black beans.
3. Remove the lid and stir in the olives and black beans. Add the salt, pepper, and marinara sauce and stir. Simmer for 5 minutes, uncovered.
4. Remove from the heat and serve immediately or let cool and divide the mixture evenly among 4 meal prep containers.

**PER SERVING**

Calories: 402|Protein: 17g | Carbs: 70g | Fiber: 14g | Sugars: 12g | Fat: 6g

## Whitefish with Lemon and Capers

**Prep time: 5 minutes | Cook time: 20 minutes | Serves 4**

- 4 (4- to 5-ounce) cod fillets (or any whitefish)
- 1 tablespoon extra-virgin olive oil
- 1 teaspoon salt, divided
- 4 tablespoons (½ stick) unsalted butter
- 2 tablespoons capers, drained
- 3 tablespoons lemon juice
- ½ teaspoon freshly ground black pepper

1. Preheat the oven to 450°F. Put the cod in a large baking dish and drizzle with the olive oil and ½ teaspoon of salt. Bake for 15 minutes.
2. Right before the fish is done cooking, melt the butter in a small saucepan over medium heat. Add the capers, lemon juice, remaining ½ teaspoon of salt, and pepper, simmer for 30 seconds.
3. Place the fish in a serving dish once it is done baking | spoon the caper sauce over the fish and serve.

**PER SERVING**

Calories: 255 | Protein: 26g | Carbs: 1g | Sugars: 0g | Fiber: 0g | Fat: 16g

## Grilled Salmon

**Prep time: 5 minutes | Cook time: 10 minutes | Serves 4**

- 1 teaspoon garlic powder
- 1 teaspoon onion powder
- 1 teaspoon freshly ground black pepper
- ½ teaspoon salt
- 4 (5- to 6-ounce) salmon fillets with skin on
- ½ cup lemon juice

1. In a small bowl, mix together the garlic powder, onion powder, black pepper, and salt.
2. Put the salmon in a large dish and pour the lemon juice over the salmon.
3. Season the salmon with the seasoning mix.
4. Preheat a grill, grill pan, or lightly oiled skillet to high heat. Place the salmon on the grill or skillet, skin-side down first.
5. Cook each side for 4 minutes. Serve immediately.

**PER SERVING**

Calories: 238 | Protein: 29g | Carbs: 4g | Sugars: 1g | Fiber: 0g | Fat: 13g

## Lemon Orzo with Fresh Herbs

**Prep time: 10 minutes | Cook time: 10 minutes | Serves 4**

- 2 cups orzo
- ½ cup fresh parsley, finely chopped
- ½ cup fresh basil, finely chopped
- 2 tablespoons lemon zest
- ½ cup extra-virgin olive oil
- ⅓ cup lemon juice
- 1 teaspoon salt
- ½ teaspoon freshly ground black pepper

1. Bring a large pot of water to a boil. Add the orzo and cook for 7 minutes. Drain and rinse with cold water. Let the orzo sit in a strainer to completely drain and cool.
2. Once the orzo has cooled, put it in a large bowl and add the parsley, basil, and lemon zest.
3. In a small bowl, whisk together the olive oil, lemon juice, salt, and pepper. Add the dressing to the pasta and toss everything together. Serve at room temperature or chilled.

**PER SERVING**

Calories: 568 | Protein: 11g | Carbs: 65g | Sugars: 4g | Fiber: 4g | Fat: 29g

## Quick Shrimp Fettuccine

**Prep time: 10 minutes | Cook time: 10 minutes | Serves 4-6**

- 8 ounces fettuccine pasta
- ¼ cup extra-virgin olive oil
- 3 tablespoons garlic, minced
- 1 pound large shrimp (21-25), peeled and deveined
- ⅓ cup lemon juice
- 1 tablespoon lemon zest
- ½ teaspoon salt
- ½ teaspoon freshly ground black pepper

1. Bring a large pot of salted water to a boil. Add the fettuccine and cook for 8 minutes.
2. In a large saucepan over medium heat, cook the olive oil and garlic for 1 minute.
3. Add the shrimp to the saucepan and cook for 3 minutes on each side. Remove the shrimp from the pan and set aside.
4. Add the lemon juice and lemon zest to the saucepan, along with the salt and pepper.
5. Reserve ½ cup of the pasta water and drain the pasta.
6. Add the pasta water to the saucepan with the lemon juice and zest and stir everything together. Add the pasta and toss together to evenly coat the pasta. Transfer the pasta to a serving dish and top with the cooked shrimp. Serve warm.

**PER SERVING**

Calories: 615 | Protein: 33g | Carbs: 89g | Sugars: 3g | Fiber: 4g | Fat: 17g

### Seasoned Tuna Steaks

**Prep time:** 5 minutes | **Cook time:** 9 minutes | **Serves 4**

- 1 teaspoon garlic powder
- ½ teaspoon salt
- ¼ teaspoon dried thyme
- ¼ teaspoon dried oregano
- 4 tuna steaks
- 2 tablespoons olive oil
- 1 lemon, quartered

1. Preheat the air fryer to 380°F.
2. In a small bowl, whisk together the garlic powder, salt, thyme, and oregano.
3. Coat the tuna steaks with olive oil. Season both sides of each steak with the seasoning blend. Place the steaks in a single layer in the air fryer basket.
4. Cook for 5 minutes, then flip and cook for an additional 3 to 4 minutes.

**PER SERVING**

Calories: 269 | Fat: 14g | Protein: 33g | Carbs: 1g | Fiber: 0g | Sugar: 0g

### Chicken Shawarma

**Prep time:** 10 minutes | **Cook time:** 15 minutes | **Serves 4**

- 1 pound boneless skinless chicken breasts, cubed
- ¼ cup nonfat plain Greek yogurt
- 2 tablespoons olive oil
- 1 teaspoon dried oregano
- 1 teaspoon ground cumin
- 1 teaspoon ground cinnamon
- 1 teaspoon salt
- ¼ teaspoon ground turmeric
- ¼ teaspoon black pepper
- Rice, for serving (optional)
- Greek salad, for serving (optional)
- Tzatziki sauce, for serving (optional)

1. Preheat the air fryer to 380°F.
2. In a large bowl, combine all ingredients and mix together until the chicken is coated well.
3. Spread the chicken mixture in an even layer in the air fryer basket, then cook for 10 minutes. Stir the chicken mixture and cook for an additional 5 minutes.
4. Serve with rice, a Greek salad, and tzatziki sauce.

**PER SERVING**

Calories: 209 | Fat: 10g | Protein: 27g | Carbs: 2g | Fiber: 0g | Sugar: 1g

## Balsamic Black Beans

Prep time: 5 minutes | Cook time: 20 minutes | Serves 5

- 1 teaspoon extra-virgin olive oil or vegetable broth
- ½ cup diced sweet onion
- 1 teaspoon ground cumin
- 1 teaspoon ground cardamom (optional)
- 2 (14.5-ounce) cans black beans, rinsed and drained
- ¼ to ½ cup vegetable broth
- 2 tablespoons balsamic vinegar

1. In a large pot over medium-high heat, heat the olive oil. Add the onion, cumin, and cardamom (if using) and sauté for 3 to 5 minutes, until the onion is translucent. Add the beans and ¼ cup broth, and bring to a boil. Add up to ½ cup more of broth for "soupier" beans. Cover, reduce the heat, and simmer for 10 minutes.
2. Add the balsamic vinegar, increase the heat to medium-high, and cook for 3 more minutes uncovered.
3. Transfer to a large storage container, or divide the beans evenly among 5 single-serving storage containers. Let cool before sealing the lids.

**PER SERVING**

Calories: 200 | Fat: 2g | Protein: 13g | Carbs: 34g | Fiber: 12g | Sugar: 1g

## Cannellini Bean Lettuce Wraps

Prep time: 10 minutes | Cook time: 10 minutes | Serves 4

- 1 tablespoon extra-virgin olive oil
- ½ cup diced red onion (about ¼ onion)
- ¾ cup chopped fresh tomatoes (about 1 medium tomato)
- ¼ teaspoon freshly ground black pepper
- 1 (15-ounce) can cannellini or great northern beans, drained and rinsed
- ¼ cup finely chopped fresh curly parsley
- ½ cup Lemony Garlic Hummus or ½ cup prepared hummus
- 8 romaine lettuce leaves

1. In a large skillet over medium heat, heat the oil. Add the onion and cook for 3 minutes, stirring occasionally. Add the tomatoes and pepper and cook for 3 more minutes, stirring occasionally. Add the beans and cook for 3 more minutes, stirring occasionally. Remove from the heat, and mix in the parsley.
2. Spread 1 tablespoon of hummus over each lettuce leaf. Evenly spread the warm bean mixture down the center of each leaf. Fold one side of the lettuce leaf over the filling lengthwise, then fold over the other side to make a wrap and serve.

**PER SERVING**

Calories: 188 | Fat: 5g | Carbs: 28 g | Fiber: 9g | Protein 10g | Sugar 2g

### Crispy Garlic Sliced Eggplant

**Prep time: 5 minutes | Cook time: 25 minutes | Serves 4**

- 1 egg
- 1 tablespoon water
- ½ cup whole wheat bread crumbs
- 1 teaspoon garlic powder
- ½ teaspoon dried oregano
- ½ teaspoon salt
- ½ teaspoon paprika
- 1 medium eggplant, sliced into ¼-inch-thick rounds
- 1 tablespoon olive oil

1. Preheat the air fryer to 360°F.
2. In a medium shallow bowl, beat together the egg and water until frothy.
3. In a separate medium shallow bowl, mix together bread crumbs, garlic powder, oregano, salt, and paprika.
4. Dip each eggplant slice into the egg mixture, then into the bread crumb mixture, coating the outside with crumbs. Place the slices in a single layer in the bottom of the air fryer basket.
5. Drizzle the tops of the eggplant slices with the olive oil, then fry for 15 minutes. Turn each slice and cook for an additional 10 minutes.

**PER SERVING**

Calories: 137 | Fat: 5g | Protein: 5g | Carbs: 19g | Fiber: 5g | Sugar: 6g

### Lemon-Pepper Chicken Thighs

**Prep time: 5 minutes | Cook time: 22 minutes | Serves 4**

- 4 bone-in chicken thighs, skin and fat removed
- 2 tablespoons olive oil
- 1 teaspoon garlic powder
- 1 teaspoon salt
- Black pepper
- 1 lemon, sliced

1. Preheat the air fryer to 380°F.
2. Coat the chicken thighs in the olive oil, garlic powder, and salt.
3. Tear off four pieces of aluminum foil, with each sheet being large enough to envelop one chicken thigh.
4. Place one chicken thigh onto each piece of foil, season it with black pepper, and then top it with slices of lemon.
5. Bake for 20 to 22 minutes, or until the internal temperature of the chicken has reached 165°F.
6. Remove the foil packets from the air fryer. Carefully open each packet to avoid a steam burn.

**PER SERVING**

Calories: 480 | Fat: 38g | Protein: 31g | Carbs: 1g | Fiber: 0g | Sugar: 0g

## Lemon and Paprika Herb-Marinated Chicken

Prep time: 10 minutes, plus 30 minutes to marinate | Cook time: 15 minutes | Serves 2

- 2 tablespoons olive oil
- 4 tablespoons freshly squeezed lemon juice
- ¼ teaspoon salt
- 1 teaspoon paprika
- 1 teaspoon dried basil
- ½ teaspoon dried thyme
- ¼ teaspoon garlic powder
- 2 (4-ounce) boneless, skinless chicken breasts

1. In a bowl with a lid, combine the olive oil, lemon juice, salt, paprika, basil, thyme, and garlic powder.
2. Add the chicken and marinate for at least 30 minutes, or up to 4 hours.
3. When ready to cook, heat the grill to medium-high (about 350–400°F) and oil the grill grate. Alternately, you can also cook these in a nonstick sauté pan over medium-high heat.
4. Grill the chicken for 6 to 7 minutes, or until it lifts away from the grill easily. Flip it over and grill for another 6 to 7 minutes, or until it reaches an internal temperature of 165°F.

**PER SERVING**

Calories: 252 | Fat: 16g | Carbs: 2g | Fiber: 1g | Sugar: 1g | Protein: 27g

## Italian Tuna Sandwiches

Prep time: 10 minutes | Cook time: 0 minutes| Serves 4

- 3 tablespoons freshly squeezed lemon juice (from 1 medium lemon)
- 2 tablespoons extra-virgin olive oil
- 1 garlic clove, minced (about ½ teaspoon)
- ½ teaspoon freshly ground black pepper
- 2 (5-ounce) cans tuna, drained
- 1 (2.25-ounce) can sliced olives, any green or black variety (about ½ cup)
- ½ cup chopped fresh fennel, including fronds, or celery (about 1 stalk), including leaves
- 8 slices whole-grain crusty bread

1. In a medium bowl, whisk to combine the lemon juice, oil, garlic, and pepper. Add the tuna, olives, and fennel. Using a fork, separate the tuna into chunks and stir to combine all the ingredients.
2. Divide the tuna salad equally among 4 slices of bread. Top each with the remaining bread slices. Let the sandwiches sit for at least 5 minutes so the zesty filling can soak into the bread before serving.

**PER SERVING**

Calories: 952 | Fat: 17g | Carbs: 37 g | Fiber: 7g | Protein 165g | Sugar 6g

# Chapter 7

## Simple Sides and Salads

## Chicken, Spinach, and Berry Salad

**Prep time: 5 minutes | Cook time: none | Serves 4**

**For the Salad**
- 8 cups baby spinach
- 2 cups shredded rotisserie chicken
- ½ cup sliced strawberries or other berries
- ½ cup sliced almonds
- 1 avocado, sliced
- ¼ cup crumbled feta (optional)

**For the Dressing**
- 2 tablespoons extra-virgin olive oil
- 2 teaspoons honey
- 2 teaspoons balsamic vinegar

**To Make The Salad**
1. In a large bowl, combine the spinach, chicken, strawberries, and almonds.
2. Pour the dressing over the salad and lightly toss.
3. Divide into four equal portions and top each with sliced avocado and 1 tablespoon of crumbled feta (if using).

**To Make The Dressing**
1. In a small bowl, whisk together the olive oil, honey, and balsamic vinegar.

**PER SERVING**

Calories: 339 | Fat: 22g | Protein: 25g | Carbs: 13g | Sugars: 6g | Fiber: 6g

## Creamy Traditional Hummus

**Prep time: 5 minutes | Cook time: 15 minutes | Serves 8**

- 1 (15-ounce) can garbanzo beans, rinsed and drained
- 2 cloves garlic, peeled
- ¼ cup lemon juice
- 1 teaspoon salt
- ¼ cup plain Greek yogurt
- ½ cup tahini paste
- 2 tablespoons extra-virgin olive oil, divided

1. Add the garbanzo beans, garlic cloves, lemon juice, and salt to a food processor fitted with a chopping blade. Blend for 1 minute, until smooth.
2. Scrape down the sides of the processor. Add the Greek yogurt, tahini paste, and 1 tablespoon of olive oil and blend for another minute, until creamy and well combined.
3. Spoon the hummus into a serving bowl. Drizzle the remaining tablespoon of olive oil on top.

**PER SERVING**

Calories: 189 | Protein: 7g | Carbs: 14g | Sugars: 2g | Fiber: 4g | Fat: 13g

## Balsamic Mushrooms

Prep time: 30 minutes | Cook time: 20 minutes | Serves 4

- 2 tablespoons of balsamic vinegar
- 1 lb. of mushrooms
- half teaspoon of dried parsley
- 2 tablespoons of olive oil
- 1 teaspoon of minced garlic minced
- 1/4 teaspoon of pepper
- half teaspoon of dried basil
- half teaspoon of salt

1. In a bowl, add all ingredients, except for mushrooms.
2. Mix and add mushrooms, let it rest for 20 minutes.
3. Spread on a foil lined baking sheet and roast for 20 minutes at 400°F.

**PER SERVING**

Calories: 96 | Fat: 7 g | Carbs: 5 g | Fiber: 1 g | Sugar: 3 g | Protein: 4 g

## Garlic and Herb Zoodles

Prep time: 5 to 10 minutes | Cook time: 2 minutes | Serves 4

- 1 teaspoon extra-virgin olive oil or 2 tablespoons vegetable broth
- 1 teaspoon minced garlic (about 1 clove)
- 4 medium zucchini, spiralized
- ½ teaspoon dried basil
- ½ teaspoon dried oregano
- ¼ to ½ teaspoon red pepper flakes, to taste
- ¼ teaspoon salt (optional)
- ¼ teaspoon freshly ground black pepper

1. In a large skillet over medium-high heat, heat the olive oil. Add the garlic, zucchini, basil, oregano, red pepper flakes, salt (if using), and black pepper. Sauté for 1 to 2 minutes, until barely tender.
2. Divide the zoodles evenly among 4 storage containers. Let cool before sealing the lids.

**PER SERVING**

Calories: 44 | Fat: 2g | Protein: 3g | Carbs: 7g | Fiber: 2g | Sugar: 3g

### Roasted Brussels Sprouts with Delicata Squash
**Prep time: 10 minutes | Cook time: 30 minutes | Serves 2**

- ½ pound Brussels sprouts, ends trimmed and outer leaves removed
- 1 medium delicata squash, halved lengthwise, seeded, and cut into 1-inch pieces
- 1 cup fresh cranberries
- 2 teaspoons olive oil
- Salt
- Freshly ground black pepper
- ½ cup balsamic vinegar
- 2 tablespoons roasted pumpkin seeds
- 2 tablespoons fresh pomegranate arils (seeds)

1. Preheat oven to 400°F and set the rack to the middle position. Line a sheet pan with parchment paper.
2. Combine the Brussels sprouts, squash, and cranberries in a large bowl. Drizzle with olive oil, and season liberally with salt and pepper. Toss well to coat and arrange in a single layer on the sheet pan.
3. Roast for 30 minutes, turning vegetables halfway through, or until Brussels sprouts turn brown and crisp in spots and squash has golden-brown spots.
4. While vegetables are roasting, prepare the balsamic glaze by simmering the vinegar for 10 to 12 minutes, or until mixture has reduced to about ¼ cup and turns a syrupy consistency.
5. Remove the vegetables from the oven, drizzle with balsamic syrup, and sprinkle with pumpkin seeds and pomegranate arils before serving.

**PER SERVING**

Calories: 201 | Fat: 7g | Carbs: 21g | Fiber: 8g | Sugar: 8g | Protein: 6g

## Citrus Green Beans with Red Onions

Prep time: 5 minutes | Cook time: 10 minutes | Serves 6

- 1 pound fresh green beans, trimmed
- ½ red onion, sliced
- 2 tablespoons olive oil
- ½ teaspoon salt
- ¼ teaspoon black pepper
- 1 tablespoon lemon juice
- Lemon wedges, for serving

1. Preheat the air fryer to 360°F. In a large bowl, toss the green beans, onion, olive oil, salt, pepper, and lemon juice until combined.
2. Pour the mixture into the air fryer and roast for 5 minutes. Stir well and roast for 5 minutes more.
3. Serve with lemon wedges.

**PER SERVING**

Calories: 67 | Fat: 5g | Saturated Fat: 1g | Protein: 1g | Carbs: 6g | Fiber: 2g | Sugar: 3g

## Garlic-Roasted Tomatoes and Olives

Prep time: 5 minutes | Cook time: 20 minutes | Serves 6

- 2 cups cherry tomatoes
- 4 garlic cloves, roughly chopped
- ½ red onion, roughly chopped
- 1 cup black olives
- 1 cup green olives
- 1 tablespoon fresh basil, minced
- 1 tablespoon fresh oregano, minced
- 2 tablespoons olive oil
- ¼ to ½ teaspoon salt

1. Preheat the air fryer to 380°F.
2. In a large bowl, combine all of the ingredients and toss together so that the tomatoes and olives are coated well with the olive oil and herbs.
3. Pour the mixture into the air fryer basket, and roast for 10 minutes. Stir the mixture well, then continue roasting for an additional 10 minutes.
4. Remove from the air fryer, transfer to a serving bowl, and enjoy.

**PER SERVING**

Calories: 109 | Fat: 10g | Protein: 1g | Carbs: 6g | Fiber: 2g | Sugar: 2g

*The Good Energy Cookbook*

## Dried Apple Rings

Prep time: 20 minutes | Cook time: 5 hours | Serves 4-6

- 3 pounds of peeled apples, cut into 0.1-inches of rings
- 1 teaspoon of salt
- 1.7 ounces of lemon juice

1. In a bowl, add 3 cups of water, lemon juice and salt. Mix well.
2. Add the rings to the lemon water, let it rest for ten minutes.
3. Take the rings out and drain them on a paper towel.
4. Lay 2 layers of cheesecloth on a cooling rack, place the slices on top and place the rack on the cooking grate.
5. Place the entire set up in the cold oven at 125 F. As the temperature reaches, keep the oven door open slightly.
6. Change the temperature to 150 F.
7. Let the apples dry for 5 hours, with the door slightly open. Cool completely before serving.

**PER SERVING**

Calories: 21 | Fat: 0 g | Carbs: 2 g | Fiber: 2 g | Sugar: 3.2 g | Protein: 0 g

## Citrusy Spinach Salad

Prep time: 10 minutes | Cook time: 5 minutes | Serves 4

- 1 large ripe tomato
- 1 medium red onion
- ½ teaspoon fresh lemon zest
- 3 tablespoons balsamic vinegar
- ¼ cup extra-virgin olive oil
- ½ teaspoon salt
- 1 pound baby spinach, washed, stems removed

1. Dice the tomato into ¼-inch pieces and slice the onion into long slivers.
2. In a small bowl, whisk together the lemon zest, balsamic vinegar, olive oil, and salt.
3. Put the spinach, tomatoes, and onions in a large bowl. Pour the dressing over the salad and lightly toss to coat.

**PER SERVING**

Calories: 172 | Protein: 4g | Carbs: 10g | Sugars: 2g | Fiber: 4g | Fat: 1

# Chapter 8

## Nutritious Soups and Stews

## Cauliflower and Broccoli Soup

**Prep time: 10 minutes | Cook time: 30 minutes | Serves 5**

- 1 tbsp olive oil
- 1 large onion, chopped
- 3 garlic cloves, minced
- 1 head cauliflower, chopped
- 1 head broccoli, chopped
- 4 cups low-sodium vegetable broth
- 2 cups water
- 1/2 cup unsweetened almond milk
- 1 tsp dried dill
- salt and pepper, to taste

1. Heat olive oil in a large pot over medium heat. Add onion and garlic, cook until softened.
2. Add cauliflower and broccoli, stirring for 5 minutes.
3. Pour in broth, water, and dill. Bring to a boil, then simmer for 20 minutes or until vegetables are tender.
4. Blend the soup until smooth. Stir in almond milk, and season with salt and pepper.

**PER SERVING**

Calories: 140 | Protein: 6g | Carbs: 18g | Fiber: 7g | Sugars: 5g | Fat: 4g

## Butternut Squash Soup

**Prep time: 10 minutes | Cook time: 45 minutes | Serves 6**

- 1 sweet chopped onion
- 3 lbs. of peeled butternut squash, chopped
- 1 diced carrot
- 1 sprig of fresh thyme
- 1 diced celery rib
- 1 tablespoon of olive oil
- 1 sprig of fresh rosemary
- 1/4 teaspoon of black pepper
- 3 cups of vegetable broth
- 1 peeled, chopped apple
- 3 minced garlic cloves
- 1/4 teaspoon of ground cinnamon
- 1 teaspoon of kosher salt

1. Sauté garlic, celery, carrots and onion for 3-5 minutes.
2. Add the rest of the ingredients and cook until squash is tender for 20-30 minutes; add more broth if it gets dry.
3. with a stick blender, puree the soup and adjust seasoning.
4. Serve.

**PER SERVING**

Calories: 159 | Fat: 3 g | Carbs: 36 g | Fiber: 6 g | Sugar: 10 g | Protein: 3 g

## Cauliflower Leek Soup

Prep time: 10 minutes | Cook time: 20 minutes | Serves 2

- Avocado oil cooking spray
- 2½ cups chopped leeks (2 to 3 leeks)
- 2½ cups cauliflower florets
- 1 garlic clove, peeled
- ⅓ cup low-sodium vegetable broth
- ½ cup half-and-half
- ¼ teaspoon salt
- ¼ teaspoon freshly ground black pepper

1. Heat a large stockpot over medium-low heat. When hot, coat the cooking surface with cooking spray. Put the leeks and cauliflower into the pot.
2. Increase the heat to medium and cover the pan. Cook for 10 minutes, stirring halfway through.
3. Add the garlic and cook for 5 minutes.
4. Add the broth and deglaze the pan, stirring to scrape up the browned bits from the bottom.
5. Transfer the broth and vegetables to a food processor or blender and add the half-and-half, salt, and pepper. Blend well.

**PER SERVING**

Calories: 173 | Fat: 7g | Protein: 6g | Carbs: 24g | Sugars: 8g | Fiber: 5g

## Tomato Basil Soup

Prep time: 10 minutes | Cook time: 35 minutes | Serves 4

- 2 tbsp olive oil
- 1 medium onion, diced
- 4 garlic cloves, minced
- 2 cans (14.5 oz each) no-salt-added diced tomatoes
- 2 cups low-sodium vegetable broth
- 1/2 cup fresh basil leaves, chopped
- 1 tsp dried oregano
- 1/2 cup unsweetened almond milk
- salt and pepper, to taste

1. Heat olive oil in a large pot over medium heat. Sauté onion and garlic until soft.
2. Add tomatoes, broth, basil, and oregano. Bring to a boil, then reduce heat and simmer for 25 minutes.
3. Blend soup until smooth using an immersion blender. Stir in almond milk, and season with salt and pepper.

**PER SERVING**

Calories: 130 | Protein: 3g | Carbs: 18g | Fiber: 5g | Sugars: 8g | Fat: 6g

## Easy Brown Lentil Soup

**Prep time: 25 minutes | Cook time: 1 hour 20 minutes | Serves 6-8**

- 10 cups water
- 2 cups brown lentils, picked over and rinsed
- 2 teaspoons salt, divided
- ¼ cup long-grain rice, rinsed
- 3 tablespoons extra-virgin olive oil
- 1 large onion, chopped
- 2 medium potatoes, peeled
- 1 teaspoon ground cumin
- ½ teaspoon freshly ground black pepper

1. In a large pot over medium heat, bring the water, lentils, and 1 teaspoon of salt to a simmer and continue to cook, stirring occasionally, for 30 minutes.
2. At the 30-minute mark, add the rice to the lentils. Cover and continue to simmer, stirring occasionally, for another 30 minutes.
3. Remove the pot from the heat and, using a handheld immersion blender, blend the lentils and rice for 1 to 2 minutes until smooth.
4. Return the pot to the stove over low heat.
5. In a small skillet over medium heat, cook the olive oil and onions for 5 minutes until the onions are golden brown. Add the onions to the soup.
6. Cut the potatoes into ¼-inch pieces and add them to the soup.
7. Add remaining 1 teaspoon of salt, cumin, and black pepper to the soup. Stir and continue to cook for 10 to 15 minutes, or until potatoes are thoroughly cooked. Serve warm.

**PER SERVING**

Calories: 348 | Protein: 18g | Carbs: 53g | Sugars: 4g | Fiber: 20g | Fat: 9g

# Chapter 9

## Refreshing Snacks and Desserts

## Almond Joys

**Prep time: 10 minutes, plus 30 minutes to set | Cook time: 0 minutes | Serves 6**

- 1/2 cup finely shredded unsweetened dried coconut
- 1/4 cup canned coconut milk
- 2 tbsp almond flour
- 1/4 tsp coconut sugar
- 1/2 cup dairy-free dark chocolate chips (60–80% cacao)
- 18 almonds

1. Line a standard size 6-cup muffin pan with paper baking cups. Set aside. In a small bowl, combine the dried coconut, coconut milk, almond flour, and coconut sugar. Stir until well mixed.
2. Using a tablespoon measure, divide the coconut mixture into 6 balls, and flatten them with your hand to create patties. Place in the freezer while preparing the melted chocolate.
3. In a small saucepan or double boiler, melt the chocolate over medium-low heat. Stir continuously until fully melted, about 1 minute. Add about 1 tsp of melted chocolate to each of the 6 baking cups. Tilt the pan until the bottoms of the cups are fully coated with chocolate.
4. Remove the coconut patties from the freezer and place one in each cup on top of the chocolate. (The patty should be almost the same diameter as the baking cup.) Place 3 almonds on top of each coconut patty. Finish by pouring the rest of the chocolate over the almonds and coconut. Tilt and gently shake the pan to spread the chocolate evenly.
5. Place in the freezer until set, about 30 minutes.

**PER SERVING**

Calories: 178 | Protein: 2g | Carbs: 11g | Fiber: 3g | Sugars: 7g | Fat: 14g

## Twice-Baked Chips

Prep time: 2 minutes | Cook time: 30 minutes | Serves 8

- 6 baked potatoes, about 7oz each, fully cooled
- 2 tbsp olive oil
- 1 tsp salt
- 1 tsp freshly ground black pepper
- 1 tsp dried herbs (optional), such as an Italian seasoning blend

1. Line a baking sheet with parchment paper. Cut the cooled baked potatoes lengthwise into $\frac{1}{4}$-inch (6mm) slices. (They are easiest to cut when cold.) Arrange them on the prepared baking sheet in a single layer. Drizzle the olive oil over the potatoes and use your fingers to spread it over each slice. Sprinkle the potatoes with salt, pepper, and dried herbs.
2. Set the broiler to high. Place the potatoes under the broiler. After 5 minutes, begin checking for browning. Once the tops are well browned (but not burned), remove the baking sheet, carefully flip over each slice, and return to the broiler for another 5–10 minutes, or until desired crispiness is reached. Serve immediately.

**PER SERVING**

Calories: 183 | Protein: 4g | Carbs: 35g | Fiber: 3g | Sugars: 1g | Fat: 3g

## Apple Pockets

Prep time: 5 minutes | Cook time: 15 minutes | Serves 6

- 1 organic puff pastry, rolled out, at room temperature
- 1 Gala apple, peeled and sliced
- ¼ cup brown sugar
- ⅛ teaspoon ground cinnamon
- ⅛ teaspoon ground cardamom
- Nonstick cooking spray
- Honey, for topping

1. Preheat the oven to 350°F.
2. Cut the pastry dough into 4 even discs. Peel and slice the apple. In a small bowl, toss the slices with brown sugar, cinnamon, and cardamom.
3. Spray a muffin tin very well with nonstick cooking spray. Be sure to spray only the muffin holders you plan to use.
4. Once sprayed, line the bottom of the muffin tin with the dough and place 1 or 2 broken apple slices on top. Fold the remaining dough over the apple and drizzle with honey.
5. Bake for 15 minutes or until brown and bubbly.

**PER SERVING**

Calories: 250 | Protein: 3g | Carbs: 30g | Sugars: 9g | Fiber: 1g | Fat: 15g

*The Good Energy Cookbook*

## Orange Olive Oil Mug Cakes

**Prep time:** 10 minutes | **Cook time:** 2 minutes | **Serves 3**

- 6 tablespoons flour
- 2 tablespoons sugar
- ½ teaspoon baking powder
- Pinch salt
- 1 teaspoon orange zest
- 2 eggs
- 2 tablespoons olive oil
- 2 tablespoons freshly squeezed orange juice
- 2 tablespoons milk
- ½ teaspoon orange extract
- ½ teaspoon vanilla extract

1. In a small bowl, combine the flour, sugar, baking powder, salt, and orange zest.
2. In a separate bowl, whisk together the egg, olive oil, orange juice, milk, orange extract, and vanilla extract.
3. Pour the dry ingredients into the wet ingredients and stir to combine. The batter will be thick.
4. Divide the mixture into two small mugs that hold at least 6 ounces each, or one 12-ounce mug.
5. Microwave each mug separately. The small ones should take about 60 seconds, and one large mug should take about 90 seconds, but microwaves can vary. The cake will be done when it pulls away from the sides of the mug.

**PER SERVING**

Calories: 302 | Fat: 17g | Carbs: 33g | Fiber: 1g | Sugar: 14g | Protein: 6g

## Stuffed Cucumber Cups

**Prep time: 5 minutes | Cook time: 15 minutes | Serves 2**

- 1 medium cucumber (about 8 ounces, 8 to 9 inches long)
- ½ cup hummus (any flavor) or white bean dip
- 4 or 5 cherry tomatoes, sliced in half
- 2 tablespoons fresh basil, minced

1. Slice the ends off the cucumber (about ½ inch from each side) and slice the cucumber into 1-inch pieces.
2. With a paring knife or a spoon, scoop most of the seeds from the inside of each cucumber piece to make a cup, being careful to not cut all the way through.
3. Fill each cucumber cup with about 1 tablespoon of hummus or bean dip.
4. Top each with a cherry tomato half and a sprinkle of fresh minced basil.

**PER SERVING**

Calories: 135 | Fat: 6g | Carbs: 16g | Fiber: 5g | Sugar: 4g | Protein: 6g

## Savory Mediterranean Popcorn

**Prep time: 5 minutes | Cook time: 2 minutes | Serves 6**

- 3 tablespoons extra-virgin olive oil
- ¼ teaspoon garlic powder
- ¼ teaspoon freshly ground black pepper
- ¼ teaspoon sea salt
- ⅛ teaspoon dried thyme
- ⅛ teaspoon dried oregano
- 12 cups plain popped popcorn

1. In a large sauté pan or skillet, heat the oil over medium heat, until shimmering, and then add the garlic powder, pepper, salt, thyme, and oregano until fragrant.
2. In a large bowl, drizzle the oil over the popcorn, toss, and serve.

**PER SERVING**

Calories: 183 | Protein: 3g | Carbs: 19g | Sugars: 0g | Fiber: 4g | Fat: 12g

### Banana-Nut Bread Bars

**Prep time: 5 minutes | Cook time: 30 minutes | Serves 10**

- Nonstick cooking spray (optional)
- 2 large ripe bananas
- 1 tablespoon maple syrup
- ½ teaspoon vanilla extract
- 2 cups old-fashioned rolled oats
- ½ teaspoons salt
- ¼ cup chopped walnuts

1. Preheat the oven to 350°F. Lightly coat a 9-by-9-inch baking pan with nonstick cooking spray (if using) or line with parchment paper for oil-free baking.
2. In a medium bowl, mash the bananas with a fork. Add the maple syrup and vanilla extract and mix well. Add the oats, salt, and walnuts, mixing well.
3. Transfer the batter to the baking pan and bake for 25 to 30 minutes, until the top is crispy.
4. Cool completely before slicing into 9 bars. Transfer to an airtight storage container or a large plastic bag.

**PER SERVING**

Calories: 73 | Fat: 1g | Protein: 2g | Carbs: 15g | Fiber: 2g | Sugar: 5g

### Crunchy Flax and Almond Crackers

**Prep time: 15 minutes | Cook time: 60 minutes | Serves 12**

- 1/2 cup ground flaxseeds
- 1/2 cup almond flour
- 1 tablespoon coconut flour
- 2 tablespoons shelled hemp seeds
- 1/4 teaspoon sunflower seeds
- 1 egg white
- 2 tablespoons unsalted almond butter, melted

1. Warmth your oven to 300 °F. Line a baking sheet with parchment paper, keep it on the side. Add flax, almond, coconut flour, hemp seed, seeds to a bowl and mix. Add egg white and melted almond butter, mix until combined.
2. Set dough to a sheet of parchment paper and cover with another sheet of paper. Roll out dough. Cut into crackers and bake for 60 minutes. Let them cool and enjoy!

**PER SERVING**

Calories: 143 | Fat: 11 g | Carbs: 3 g | Sugars 1.7 g | Protein: 11 g| Fiber: 2.3g

## Herbed Labneh Vegetable Parfaits

**Prep time: 15 minutes | Cook time: 15 minutes | Serves 2**

For The Labneh:
- 8 ounces plain Greek yogurt (full-fat works best)
- Generous pinch salt
- 1 teaspoon za'atar seasoning
- 1 teaspoon freshly squeezed lemon juice
- Pinch lemon zest

For The Parfaits:
- ½ cup peeled, chopped cucumber
- ½ cup grated carrots
- ½ cup cherry tomatoes, halved

To Make The Labneh:
1. Line a strainer with cheesecloth and place it over a bowl.
2. Stir together the Greek yogurt and salt and place in the cheesecloth. Wrap it up and let it sit for 24 hours in the refrigerator.
3. When ready, unwrap the labneh and place it into a clean bowl. Stir in the za'atar, lemon juice, and lemon zest.

To Make The Parfaits:
1. Divide the cucumber between two clear glasses.
2. Top each portion of cucumber with about 3 tablespoons of labneh.
3. Divide the carrots between the glasses.
4. Top with another 3 tablespoons of the labneh.
5. Top parfaits with the cherry tomatoes.

**PER SERVING**

Calories: 143 | Fat: 7g | Carbs: 16g | Fiber: 2g | Sugar: 13g | Protein: 5g

## Garlic Crispy Smashed Potatoes

Prep time: 20 minutes | Cook time: 1 hour and 30 minutes | Serves 6

**Potatoes:**
- 2 tablespoons of olive oil
- 12 Yukon small gold potatoes
- sea salt, fresh parsley & black pepper, to taste

**Cashew Cream:**
- 1 whole bulb of Garlic
- 2 tablespoons of fresh chives
- 3/4 cup of soaked Cashews
- 1 tablespoon of lemon juice

1. Let the oven preheat to 400 F.
2. Peel any outer papery layer of garlic, cut the top off the only ¼". Coat in olive oil and wrap in foil.
3. Place in the oven, bake for 40 to 50 minutes.
4. In a food processor, add drained cashews with a little bit of hot water and pulse until smooth. Add the roasted peeled garlic, chives and the rest of the ingredients. Pulse until smooth.
5. Boil potatoes for 8 to 10 minutes. Drain and dry the potatoes, transfer on a baking sheet.
6. Lightly smash with glass, add oil, salt and pepper.
7. Bake for half an hour until crispy and golden. Take the tray out, drizzle with olive oil, broil for 5 minutes.

**PER SERVING**

Calories: 328 | Fat: 12 g | Carbs: 38 g | Fiber: 9 g | Sugar: 5 g | Protein: 11 g

# Appendix 1 Measurement Conversion Chart

| Volume Equivalents (Dry) ||
|---|---|
| US STANDARD | METRIC (APPROXIMATE) |
| 1/8 teaspoon | 0.5 mL |
| 1/4 teaspoon | 1 mL |
| 1/2 teaspoon | 2 mL |
| 3/4 teaspoon | 4 mL |
| 1 teaspoon | 5 mL |
| 1 tablespoon | 15 mL |
| 1/4 cup | 59 mL |
| 1/2 cup | 118 mL |
| 3/4 cup | 177 mL |
| 1 cup | 235 mL |
| 2 cups | 475 mL |
| 3 cups | 700 mL |
| 4 cups | 1 L |

| Volume Equivalents (Liquid) |||
|---|---|---|
| US STANDARD | US STANDARD (OUNCES) | METRIC (APPROXIMATE) |
| 2 tablespoons | 1 fl.oz. | 30 mL |
| 1/4 cup | 2 fl.oz. | 60 mL |
| 1/2 cup | 4 fl.oz. | 120 mL |
| 1 cup | 8 fl.oz. | 240 mL |
| 1 1/2 cup | 12 fl.oz. | 355 mL |
| 2 cups or 1 pint | 16 fl.oz. | 475 mL |
| 4 cups or 1 quart | 32 fl.oz. | 1 L |
| 1 gallon | 128 fl.oz. | 4 L |

| Weight Equivalents ||
|---|---|
| US STANDARD | METRIC (APPROXIMATE) |
| 1 ounce | 28 g |
| 2 ounces | 57 g |
| 5 ounces | 142 g |
| 10 ounces | 284 g |
| 15 ounces | 425 g |
| 16 ounces (1 pound) | 455 g |
| 1.5 pounds | 680 g |
| 2 pounds | 907 g |

| Temperatures Equivalents ||
|---|---|
| FAHRENHEIT(F) | CELSIUS(C) APPROXIMATE) |
| 225 °F | 107 °C |
| 250 °F | 120 ° °C |
| 275 °F | 135 °C |
| 300 °F | 150 °C |
| 325 °F | 160 °C |
| 350 °F | 180 °C |
| 375 °F | 190 °C |
| 400 °F | 205 °C |
| 425 °F | 220 °C |
| 450 °F | 235 °C |
| 475 °F | 245 °C |
| 500 °F | 260 °C |

# Appendix 2 The Dirty Dozen and Clean Fifteen

The Environmental Working Group (EWG) is a nonprofit, nonpartisan organization dedicated to protecting human health and the environment Its mission is to empower people to live healthier lives in a healthier environment. This organization publishes an annual list of the twelve kinds of produce, in sequence, that have the highest amount of pesticide residue-the Dirty Dozen-as well as a list of the fifteen kinds ofproduce that have the least amount of pesticide residue-the Clean Fifteen.

## THE DIRTY DOZEN

The 2016 Dirty Dozen includes the following produce. These are considered among the year's most important produce to buy organic:

| Strawberries | Spinach |
| --- | --- |
| Apples | Tomatoes |
| Nectarines | Bell peppers |
| Peaches | Cherry tomatoes |
| Celery | Cucumbers |
| Grapes | Kale/collard greens |
| Cherries | Hot peppers |

The Dirty Dozen list contains two additional itemskale/collard greens and hot peppers-because they tend to contain trace levels of highly hazardous pesticides.

## THE CLEAN FIFTEEN

The least critical to buy organically are the Clean Fifteen list. The following are on the 2016 list:

| Avocados | Papayas |
| --- | --- |
| Corn | Kiw |
| Pineapples | Eggplant |
| Cabbage | Honeydew |
| Sweet peas | Grapefruit |
| Onions | Cantaloupe |
| Asparagus | Cauliflower |
| Mangos | |

Some of the sweet corn sold in the United States are made from genetically engineered (GE) seedstock. Buy organic varieties of these crops to avoid GE produce.

# Appendix 3 Index

### A

almond butter .................................. 13, 19, 59
almond milk ................................ 13, 21, 51, 52
apple ........................................... 19, 51, 56
avocado ....................................... 24, 32, 45

### B

banana .............................................. 16, 17
basil ............... 14, 26, 30, 38, 43, 46, 48, 52, 58
beef ..................................................... 34
berries ..................................... 13, 19, 21, 45
blackberries ........................................... 16
blueberries ...................................... 17, 18, 19
butternut .......................................... 51, 60

### C

cabbage ............................................. 13, 18
cannellini ......................................... 30, 41
cardamom ....................................... 25, 41, 56
carrot .............................................. 18, 51
cauliflower ........................................ 51, 52
cheese ........................................ 22, 29, 33
cherry ...................................... 24, 34, 48, 58, 60
chicken ................................. 32, 40, 42, 43, 45
chives ................................................. 61
chocolate ............................................. 55
cilantro ............................................ 25, 61
coconut milk ................................. 16, 19, 55
cranberries ........................................... 47
cucumber ............................... 13, 17, 58, 60
cumin ........................................ 27, 40, 41, 53

### D

dill .............................................. 51, 60

### E

eggplant ......................................... 31, 42, 60
eggs ........................................ 21, 22, 24, 25, 57

### F

fennel ............................................. 43, 53
feta ........................................... 22, 45, 54
flakes ......................................... 23, 32, 46
flaxseeds ........................................ 16, 59

### G

garlic ............... 18, 22, 24, 25, 26, 27, 30, 31, 32, 33, 34, 37, 39, 40, 42, 43, 45, 46, 48, 51, 52, 58, 61
garnish ......................................... 16, 17, 33
grapes .................................................. 17
Greek yogurt ....................... 13, 16, 18, 40, 45, 60
green olives .................................... 30, 48

### H

herbs ........................................... 48, 56
honey .......................................... 45, 56, 61

### J

jalapeño ...................................... 14, 15, 54
juice .............. 15, 16, 17, 19, 30, 31, 32, 34, 37, 38, 39, 43, 45, 48, 49, 57, 60

### K

kalamata olives ................................... 36
kale ........................................ 17, 18, 24, 60
kosher salt .................................. 21, 51, 55

## L

lemon juice .............. 30, 31, 32, 34, 37, 38, 39, 43, 45, 48, 49, 60, 61
lentils ................................. 53

## M

milk .......................... 13, 16, 19, 21, 24, 51, 52, 55, 57,

## N

nutmeg ............................... 29, 60

## O

olive oil .................................. 21, 22, 25, 26, 27, 29, 30, 31, 32, 33, 34, 37, 38, 39, 40, 41, 42, 43, 45, 46, 47, 48, 49, 51, 52, 53, 56, 57, 58, 61
onion .................. 24, 27, 31, 37, 41, 48, 49, 51, 52, 53
orange juice ........................... 16, 57
oregano ........... 27, 30, 32, 34, 40, 42, 46, 48, 52, 58

## P

paprika ........................ 25, 42, 43, 55
parmesan cheese ............ 29, 57
parsley ......................... 32, 33, 38, 41, 46, 61
peanut ...................... 21, 50
pecans ...................... 23, 56
pesto ...................... 24
popcorn ...................... 58
potato ...................... 25, 27
pumpkin ...................... 23, 26, 29, 47

## Q

quinoa ...................... 24, 36

## R

raspberries ...................... 21, 55
red bell ...................... 22, 25
red onion ...................... 41, 48, 49, 61
romaine ...................... lettuce 14, 19, 41
rosemary ...................... 29, 31, 34, 51, 61

## S

salt ...................... 18, 21, 22, 23, 24, 26, 27, 29, 30, 31, 32, 33, 34, 36, 37, 38, 39, 40, 42, 43, 45, 46, 47, 48, 49, 51, 52, 53, 56, 57, 58, 59, 60, 61
shrimp ...................... 39
spinach ...................... 18, 19, 21, 24, 45, 49
stevia ...................... 16, 17
strawberries ...................... 16, 17, 18, 19, 21, 45, 60
sugar ...................... 15, 16, 55, 56, 57

## T

tahini ...................... 45
thyme ...................... 30, 33, 40, 43, 51, 58
tomato ...................... 14, 26, 41, 49, 58, 60
tuna ...................... 40, 43
turmeric ...................... 25, 40, 61

## V

vanilla ...................... 13, 16, 21, 23, 57, 59, 60

## W

walnut ...................... 21

## Y

yellow onion ...................... 27

## Z

zucchini ...................... 32, 34, 36, 46, 60

**Hey there!**

Wow, can you believe we've reached the end of this culinary journey together? I'm truly thrilled and filled with joy as I think back on all the recipes we've shared and the flavors we've discovered. This experience, blending a bit of tradition with our own unique twists, has been a journey of love for good food. and knowing you've been out there, giving these dishes a try, has made this adventure incredibly special to me.

Even though we're turning the last page of this book, I hope our conversation about all things delicious doesn't have to end. I cherish your thoughts, your experiments, and yes, even those moments when things didn't go as planned. Every piece of feedback you share is invaluable, helping to enrich this experience for us all.

I'd be so grateful if you could take a moment to share your thoughts with me, be it through a review on Amazon or any other place you feel comfortable expressing yourself online. Whether it's praise, constructive criticism, or even an idea for how we might do things differently in the future, your input is what truly makes this journey meaningful.

This book is a piece of my heart, offered to you with all the love and enthusiasm I have for cooking. But it's your engagement and your words that elevate it to something truly extraordinary.

Thank you from the bottom of my heart for being such an integral part of this culinary adventure. Your openness to trying new things and sharing your experiences has been the greatest gift.

**Catch you later,**

**Betty J. Lawson**

Betty J. Lawson

Printed in Dunstable, United Kingdom